These Broken Eggs

My Life as an Army Wife

Order this book online at www.trafford.com
or email orders@trafford.com

Most Trafford titles are also available at major online book retailers.

Note for Librarians: A cataloguing record for this book is available from Library
and Archives Canada at www.collectionscanada.ca/amicus/index-e.html

Printed in Victoria, BC, Canada.

ISBN: 978-1-4269-2348-7

*Our mission is to efficiently provide the world's finest, most comprehensive book publishing
service, enabling every author to experience success. To find out how to publish your
book, your way, and have it available worldwide, visit us online at www.trafford.com*

Trafford rev. 7/09/2010

 www.trafford.com

North America & international
toll-free: 1 888 232 4444 (USA & Canada)
phone: 250 383 6864 ♦ fax: 812 355 4082

This book is written in memory of all the World War II veterans and their wives. May their stories be told and retold.

Prologue

Our mom spent a lot of time sorting through her memories and writing this book with love. It was important to her for us to know what her life was like when she followed our dad while he was in the Army Air Force. Mom told us she wanted to have eleven chapters in her book and that she was almost finished with Chapter 11. Unfortunately, she had a stroke and wasn't able to complete the final chapter of her book. We didn't change any of her words. This is her story.

We Met At Davis Business College

Chapter One

I met my husband as I was coming down the steps of Davis Business College in Toledo, Ohio in 1938, the summer I graduated from DeVilbiss High School. My cousin, a classmate, and I were going to a nearby restaurant for lunch. He was coming up the steps dressed in a business suit and a tie, carrying a rather large briefcase and wearing a smile. As he passed us on the steps, he tipped his hat to us. When he could not hear me, I mentioned to my friends, "I know that guy, but I can't remember how I know him."

Later that summer, Davis College planned a school picnic to be held at Toledo Beach (a park area on Lake Erie with amusement rides and a dance floor built over the water). The school posted a sheet for students who needed transportation to the picnic. Five or six cars were there for us. My cousin and I were in the same car and

I noticed that Harold was there with his car and he was providing rides.

The dance floor over the water of Lake Erie was exciting and my friends were paying the nickel, or whatever the cost was, for each dance. A girlfriend and I were dancing when two fellows came to the railing outside the dance floor and asked if the two of us would go with them to ride the Ferris Wheel. One of the two boys was Harold. We talked with them for a minute and told them we would go with them after this dance was over.

We were somewhat nervous and excited and after that dance ended, we looked around but didn't see them. We laughed and giggled and talked for quite a while, not knowing just what to do. When we still didn't see them we decided to go for a ride anyway. I love riding a Ferris Wheel. Most other rides make me ill but I am not afraid of heights. The higher the better. When we were up high, near the top of the ride, we noticed the same two guys down on the ground waving up at us. What a put down! (We assumed they had found someone or something else that was more fun.)

When it was getting toward evening, the picnic was winding down and some cars had already left the park. The car we were riding in and two or three other drivers decided to go to a night club on Dixie Highway. Harold and his passengers were there. He asked me to dance a few times that night and he also asked me to go with him on a certain night to hear Benny Goodman, one of the big bands of our day, playing that week at the Trianon Ballroom in Toledo. I enjoyed dancing and talking to him and I felt that other people seemed to like him. By now I knew his name was Harold Frutiger, and that he lived in a small town nearby. So I agreed to go with him to the Trianon Ballroom to hear Benny Goodman's band.

My first date with Harold opened up a new world for me. I had never been inside the Trianon or danced to a BIG NAME BAND or been in the middle of a mob of young people crowded around the bandstand to watch the band. I was surprised to see how many DeVilbiss students were there having fun.

I realized then what a sheltered life I had in High School. Oh I had dates, went to movies, roller-skating, group parties (where the parents were home), etc. Parents of some of my friends would not let their kids go to the Trianon. I had no desire to go there at that time.

In addition to dancing, we sat at a booth and talked and drank soda pop. (Soft drinks such as pepsi or root beer are still called "pop" here in Ohio.) We exchanged ideas on lots of subjects, food we liked or didn't like, classes we had in school, etc. I learned that Harold played cello (standing on a stool) when he was in the first grade in school.

As we talked, I learned that Harold lived in Temperance, Michigan (just across the Michigan/Ohio state line). He told me that he played clarinet and tenor saxophone in local bands and he had his own dance band named "Hal Ferrell Band". I also found out that he graduated from DeVilbiss High School in 1937, and that he was in my Biology class when I was a sophomore. Then I remembered how I knew him! He was one of the older boys seated in the back of the room. I remember how they would pitch pennies every time the teacher left the room.

Soon it seemed that it was time to go home. Everything had turned out nice that night and I had a very enjoyable time on my first date with Harold. A few days later when I was hurrying to the bus line, I saw Harold sitting in his car parked near the bus. He offered me a ride and

I accepted. After that he was picking me up at my home each day to take me to Davis.

On the way downtown, I learned that when he graduated from Davis College he was looking for a job in the downtown area. It didn't take long before he was hired by Houser Chemical Company, a company selling maintenance supplies. He was hired to work in the small office (it was a very small company) and in his spare time he was expected to sell supplies to local businesses. Davis College was one of his first customers.

When he passed us on the steps that day in June, he was going up to meet with Ms. Davis, the owner of Davis Business College, to see if she needed any maintenance supplies. I also learned the reason he didn't show up to meet us at the Ferris Wheel on the day of the Davis Picnic at Toledo Beach. It was because he and the other fellow did not have enough money between them to pay for all four of us to go on the ride, so they waited and caught up with us later.

My First Job, Our Marriage And Our Honeymoon

Chapter Two

In January of 1939 I graduated from Davis College and within a short time I was hired to work for a young lawyer with a small office in downtown Toledo. I was the only secretary in his office. He paid me $10.00 a week. I really enjoyed that job. I was able to go to the courthouse in Toledo often to deliver papers or pick up some files. It was so exciting to be in that very impressive building with all the marble walls and floors.

Harold and I continued to date, going to movies every week. Often we were invited to parties or asked to do things with our DeVilbiss High School friends or people we knew or met. We enjoyed going places or spending time with others in and around Toledo.

I was not too happy with the small amount I was being paid for all the work I had to do, so I began to apply for secretarial jobs on my lunch hour. Soon I was hired at The Travelers Insurance Company. My pay was $17.50 a week and I was very satisfied with that job. There were about 12 secretaries with their desks all in one large room. The building was located in downtown Toledo. Harold was working near downtown. He was now selling maintenance supplies on straight commission. (Someone else was hired to do the inside office work.) We were able to get some time together on a planned lunch hour and we enjoyed shopping the downtown stores.

The year went by fast. Harold spent a lot of time at my home. Sometimes he was invited to come for a meal with my family and then sometimes I was invited to have dinner with his family. He had a younger brother and I had a younger sister. All of my family were members of Augsburg Lutheran Church on Sylvania Ave. Harold was an active member of Pilgrim Congregational Church across Sylvania Avenue from Augsburg. Very often he met us at church on Sunday morning. The day came when he joined Augsburg Church and became a very active member.

By now Harold was making good money at his first job. He was a "born salesman", an honest and likeable man, and true to his boss. However, his boss had seen him having lunch with a competitor in the Maintenance Supply business and later asked Harold to come into his office to talk. His boss had already decided to change his pay plan. He set up hourly wages with no commission. They had some discussion and at the end of the meeting, when Harold left the office, he was very disappointed. It was a very upsetting time in his life.

The company that was asking him to work for them, called him again to meet for lunch and he decided to talk with them again. Working conditions would be much better with this new growing company. He really liked the two young brothers who owned that company and their employees were encouraging him to make the change. He finally decided to join the sales force at The Mellocraft Company and was always happy that he did. He became Sales Manager there before he was drafted into the Army (with the promise that all of his accounts would be returned to him when he returned from the war).

By this time, when we could have a lunch hour together downtown, we started to visit jewelry stores in that area. Soon after we found an engagement ring we both liked, we were engaged. We planned to wait for some time before we set a wedding date and we both began to save our money.

Finally we set June 7, 1941 for our wedding date. It wasn't long before we began to get into all the hurry and the to-do-lists and all the things needed to be done before our wedding. The most important decision for the two of us was where we were going to live. We started looking for a house to rent or buy. We finally had two houses in West Toledo that we liked. We bought the least expensive, a small two-bedroom home at 4202 Harris St. in West Toledo (a nice street with very nice neighbors). We paid $3,500.00 for it with payments of $35.00 a month. We had a front porch, living room, dining room, two bedrooms, bathroom, kitchen, basement, garage and large back yard. We started buying furniture for our home. Also it was time for Harold to trade in his one-year-old Ford for the agreed price of $100.00 at Lee Motors, a car dealer in downtown Toledo. They had agreed to this financial set-up as a yearly event. A new car every year for $100.00 plus tax!!

With our wedding approaching, bridal showers were held for me and pictures were placed in the Toledo

Blade newspaper. We went to the courthouse to get our marriage license. My mom and dad went with us because I was only 20 years old and they had to sign for me. We stood in a long line of couples waiting to get their marriage license.

Harold knew the couple standing in front of us. He introduced me to them and explained that Bill was a customer buying maintenance supplies for his hamburger restaurant at Point Place, a small town near Toledo, and Grace was a waitress there. As we talked I learned that she was just my age. I asked her how she planned to get a marriage license without her parents. She whispered in my ear that she was going to lie about her age. We enjoyed talking to them and before we got up to the clerk to get our marriage license, we found they were getting married one week after June 7. They were going to visit friends in New York State and planning to tour the famous Watkins Glen, a sightseeing spot on one of the seven Finger Lakes in New York State.

Harold and I each had two weeks vacation from our jobs. Our plan was to go to Niagara Falls in Canada, Montreal and Quebec. We intended to return to the USA through Maine, New Hampshire, Vermont, and into New York State. We talked about our trips and we agreed if we were near Watkins Glen at noon on Tuesday, after they were married, we would meet at the post office and tour Watkins Glen together.

We did not send wedding invitations for our wedding. Back then printed invitations were not sent, at least not anywhere among our friends and families. Close relatives and friends were invited over the phone or at the showers or with a personal letter. It seemed everyone remembered the date and time. Our church was full of people by 7:00 P.M. on June 7, 1941.

I spent a lot of my wedding day shopping for some needed items at the nearby stores in West Toledo on Sylvania Ave. I was looking for crepe paper in about 2-inch or 3-inch strips to mark off the center aisle. I went to all the stores and did not find what I wanted. I stopped at the church to see that everything was ready. My Uncle Lowell and a cousin, Walter, were practicing the music they planned to sing for our wedding. Their organist was a distant cousin of my Dad. They sounded so beautiful.

I returned home later than I wanted and many of my aunts and uncles and some cousins from the country were already there and they were beginning to worry about me. Uncle Lowell and Walter arrived at my house at about the same time I did.

I was ready for my wedding in plenty of time. Our wedding attendants were all on time at the church and we finished dressing and getting our hair and makeup done in the church basement. Harold's attendants were meeting somewhere else in the church. His brother, Ken, was an usher. Another usher was his first-cousin, Chuck. My sister, Evelyn, was my maid of honor.

Everything went smooth during the service except the music. I didn't feel their singing sounded as great as it had in the afternoon. I found out later that the organist had too much liquor to drink before she came to play for our wedding. (There was no liquor, not even beer, at our house or at the reception.)

Our wedding reception was held in The Legion Hall in West Toledo. It was crowded and I don't remember much about it except that the dance band did not show up. My cousin, Jayne, who helped me so much with so many plans for our wedding, was able to get a friend to play his accordion for us that night. Big deal! We all appreciated her effort to help this one more time.

I can't remember very much about the wedding or the reception. To write this book, I phoned my sister, Evelyn, to ask her if there was anything that she could remember that would jog my memory. At first she couldn't think of a thing. She said she couldn't think of anything about her own wedding either. Later she phoned to tell me that it was at our wedding that she and her future husband, Harold's cousin Chuck, got to know each other. They were seated at the Bride's table and they spent the evening visiting with family and friends together. Chuck had returned from his Army Base to be in our wedding. He left the next morning to go back to camp. She wrote a letter to him later and the rest is history.

At the reception, it was getting late and we were encouraged to change from our wedding clothes into our 'going-away' clothes. My dad was in his car outside waiting for us. We got into the back seat and all of a sudden my mom surprised the three of us (with a last-minute decision). She decided to leave the reception and got into the front seat with Dad and we were on our way. I found out that only Harold and Dad knew where our car was parked. The friends from high school always tried to find out where the bride and groom's car was parked. They liked to decorate cars. Harold had hid our car on the second floor of the Lee Motors Company in downtown Toledo. My parents dropped us off at the car dealer's side door, we said our 'good-byes' and they drove away.

Harold had the key to unlock the old large door where cars drive in and out. We entered the empty, dimly lit building. He operated the large, rickety elevator to the second floor, turned on some lights and there was our car among the other older, used cars. We were very tired and anxious to be on our way for our honeymoon. One problem. Harold could not find the key to our car.

We were so tired. It had been a long exhausting day. We just wanted to get going. We were young and alone in a very scary second-floor with very little lighting and this was our wedding night. I was wearing my beautiful new powder blue suit and dressy heels. Harold was in his new business suit, frantically going through all his pockets to find his keys. We began to look all around our car and the other cars between the elevator and our car. We finally went back down the elevator looking for his keys. We even went outside the huge door to the street (scary as it was that time of the night to be outside in downtown Toledo). With no luck, we retraced our steps back to the second floor. I have no idea where we found the keys but somehow we did find them. Maybe the helping hand of God was with us. We were able to get the car started. We drove down on the rickety elevator and outside to the street and we were on our way to our hotel reservations at the famous Island House Hotel at Port Clinton, Ohio (on the Lake Erie about 20 or 30 miles east of Toledo).

As we entered the hotel to sign in, I remember we were very embarrassed when Harold took his handkerchief from his suit-coat pocket and rice fell out and rolled all over the lobby floor. We received our key, took the elevator up to our floor and entered our room. We had made it! We relaxed for a while and then began to unpack our bags and get ready for bed. Our room, which had hot-water radiator heat, started to get very hot. Harold began trying to adjust the heater. We couldn't stand it and finally, with no room phones in the hotel, he put on his bathrobe and went down to tell the manager to turn off the heat. The manager came into our room, did something to that heater and closed the door as he left.

The next morning we started to drive to Canada. We drove across the Thousand Island Bridge and on to Niagara Falls. We stayed in tourist homes and visited some friends as we traveled to Montreal and Quebec. We really enjoyed sightseeing and were having a wonderful honeymoon. We finally decided to return to the state of Maine. That day, traveling in Maine was relaxing. Maine was wooded and very beautiful. When we began to get tired, we started looking for a place to spend the night. We drove a long way without seeing any place to stay. Finally it was getting late in the day and we were tired and hungry. All of a sudden, we came to a place that advertised CABINS ---LODGING --- RESTAURANT.

We pulled into the driveway, rented a cabin, and unpacked our bags. A man knocked on our door. He worked at the resort and wanted to build a fire in our fireplace in our cabin, which he did. Then he told us about the restaurant, their specials for that day, their serving hours, etc. Soon we went to the restaurant and ordered the cheapest meal on the menu --- hotdog and baked beans with water cost us 99 cents each. That dinner and the cost of the cabin was the most money we paid for one night's lodging on our whole trip.

We talked about cutting our honeymoon short, but we decided we had enough money to get home if we watched our pennies. We deserved this luxurious living and we did want to spend a day at Watkins Glen on Tuesday with Harold's customers if they were there at noon. On that Tuesday at Watkins Glen, when we drove up to the Court House, Bill and Grace Merryman were there. We had a great day with them and they became two of our best friends back in Toledo. We had many good times together.

Our wonderful little home was ready for us when we arrived on Harris Street. Before we were married we moved in the furniture we bought. My parents gave us a new kitchen stove as a wedding present and we bought a new refrigerator at the same store and they were moved in before our wedding. Also a used washer was down in the basement.

We had four days of vacation time left before I needed to go back to work. Harold spent most of that Thursday and Friday visiting with his customers and his bosses. My mother came over that first day we were home. She and Dad brought all our wedding gifts which had been on display at their home. Dad went to work and Mom helped me unpack everything. When we started having too many empty boxes, packing material and wrapping paper, we started a fire in our back yard. We carried the junk, a small amount at a time, out there to burn.

We stopped for lunch and as we ate, a knock came at our back door. A man, living on the street behind us, wanted us to know that we needed to be out there at that fire. We ate our lunch around the fire! One thing I remembered as we sat there, and I began to wonder, where was the $30.00 that I had in an envelope that I took with me on our honeymoon? I never spent any of it and I forgot all about having it. I searched through all of my clothes and the purse I had for the trip and the suitcases. I finally went out to tell Mom that I couldn't find that money anywhere. We began to search in the fire and that is where we found my money. The fire had not reached it, but it was just about to burn. What a blessing!

This was my first day as a married wife in my lovely home. When Harold came home for supper, Dad had already picked up Mom and they had gone home. We had our first supper in our little kitchen, and I had a lot to tell him about my first day.

Waiting To Be Drafted

Chapter Three

Our parents didn't give us very many rules or advice about marriage either before or after we were married. All four of them were always concerned about us in a loving way. By the time we were thinking about getting married, they had become good friends. Mom Frutiger and I always got along fine together. One thing she did warn me about Harold, was that he could not wake up when his alarm clock rang in the morning. He had a terrible time turning it off and then getting out of bed.

My parents, Art and Etta (Tille) Welling, lived in West Toledo just south of the Ohio/Michigan State Line and Harold's parents, Rudy and Louise (Mager) Frutiger's small farm was about 3 miles north into Michigan. Dad Frutiger, years ago before he was married, lived in Ohio and he told us how he spent a whole day fighting the Ohio/Michigan war. On each side of the state line, they were throwing rocks back and forth at each other.

When the fight ended that day, the USA government awarded more acreage north of the state line to Ohio, and Michigan got the Upper Peninsula added to the State of Michigan.

The first morning we needed the alarm clock was the first Sunday we were home as 'man and wife'. However, we woke up before the alarm rang and we had plenty of time to eat and get ready for church. It was a thrill for me to be back in my church, seated with my family and my husband.

On Monday morning, we both needed to go back to work. Our vacation (our honeymoon) was over. Earlier, I promised myself and told Harold I was not going to turn off the alarm when it rang. I said that was his job. Our alarm rang right on time and it continued to ring. I turned over to see what was going on. There was Harold, juggling the ringing alarm in both hands high in the air, on his knees in the middle of our bed. He was working hard to keep the clock from falling from his grasp. That was Harold's first challenge in our home on Harris Avenue. He did learn, and it didn't take too long until he could wake up when the alarm rang, get up and get going without any help from me.

We never quarreled! It seemed that we always enjoyed each other and we were easy to please. (It was different after our children were born and we had different opinions about child-raising.) Now we had enough money to do and get the things we really needed. We liked each other's friends. We liked each other's families. We liked each other's company.

The thing that spoiled the peace between us was the fact that when things went wrong for me, like my cooking, accidents in and around the house, and injuries to me, I would cry. I remember, as a teenager, running up to my room at home and crying long and loud. I would stop crying long enough to listen to see if my Mom was coming up the stairs. All I wanted was for my mother to comfort me. Harold had just one reaction. Since he did not like it when I cried, he would usually look in to see what had happened. For all my small problems, he would turn around and leave the room. No arm around my shoulder. No tender words to tell me he understood. I learned from him, in a hurry, that crying didn't help. Soon I learned never to cry. I might complain but I would never cry.

When I first wore my engagement ring to work at Travelers Insurance, I knew the company policy about married women working there. Married women could only work for three months after they were married. Soon my boss called me into his office and asked me about my wedding plans. He said he didn't want to see me leave the company. I was to keep him informed of our wedding date.

In October 1941, I completed my three months at Travelers and became a stay-at-home wife. I was happy to be home all day, having fun keeping our house in good shape, plus having the freedom to do whatever I liked each day.

About then, the weather was turning cooler and we needed to get some heat in our house. We had a coal-burning furnace in the basement and that became Harold's second challenge in our little house. He did not know how to bank a coal furnace so that it kept burning all night without the fire going out before morning. This is an art that is not easy to learn and which Harold never mastered. The first thing we did when we came back from the war was to have a new beautiful gas furnace installed.

Shortly after I was home all day, we began to talk about getting a little puppy. One day my parents brought a beautiful Cocker Spaniel for us.

She was abandoned near their home. She seemed to answer to the name "Susie". The same night, when Harold came home from work, he surprised me with a puppy (a Toy Terrier). We named her "Trixie". We could not have two dogs, so we took Susie back to my parents. They loved her and she had a great home with them for many years.

When we came home from our honeymoon, we decided not to spend the money to install a telephone. We felt we didn't need one when we were both working everyday. Now that I was not working, Harold had another surprise for me. He arranged for telephone service and was able to get the phone into the house and hooked up without telling me. He went next door to call me. When the phone began to ring, I was startled! It took me a while to find where it was hidden and to answer it. What a wonderful surprise! It made me very happy.

When we were dating and many times later, Harold would tell me about the fun he had at the Boy Scout Camp on Sylvania Ave. He was a counselor there for a few years. He bragged more than once about the great food they cooked outdoors, especially how good his steak tasted.

One day I remembered and asked him if he would cook a supper for us. He said he would. We picked a day. He came home with a sack of groceries that night. When he was ready, he went into the kitchen and shut the kitchen door. I heard good things going on in the kitchen. I heard frying. I knew he was fixing steak. Finally he opened the door and escorted me to the table. There was his menu: Fried bologna with the rind on it. The edges were curled up making a cup that he had filled with green peas. He had heated a can of spaghetti. It was a pretty and colorful picture. It was all the food I like. (I still like bologna, peas and canned spaghetti.) Needless to say, he didn't fix many meals for us. (Before we married, Mark and Jayne had a grocery shower for us with all the men and women in our family attending. We had canned goods and box food for a year.) I felt the only thing Harold bought at the grocery store for our meal was the bologna.

On December 7, 1941, we were both sitting, very relaxed, together with our backs against the one arm of the davenport (sofa) listening to the radio. We had taken our shoes off and had stretched our legs and feet up on the sofa. Our president, Franklin D. Roosevelt, came on the air with another of his "Fireside Chats". He announced that our American ships had been bombed by the Japanese at Pearl Harbor. We were at war.

What a shocker that was! We didn't know what to think, what to say or do. We were numb with doubts and fear. We didn't talk much about anything that night. We were dumbfounded! We both knew that our lives were going to change.

By that Christmas and into the year 1942, we knew that Harold would probably need to go to war. What he didn't tell me was that he was talking to the different recruiters on his lunch hour about the rules for enlisting. I never did learn why he didn't tell me about this important part of our life. Maybe he thought it would be too upsetting for me, that maybe I would cry or would worry too much about it. Maybe this was something he wanted to decide for himself. When he finally knew what he wanted to do, he stopped at the draft board in West Toledo on his way home from work, to tell them he was planning to enlist soon in the U.S. Navy. The recruiters at the Navy office promised that he would be assigned to the Navy Band. (Music has always been his love.)

The Draft Board told him that he needed to go back to the Navy and sign up that day. They had his draft notice on their desk and that it would be mailed with all the others at the Post Office in a few minutes. Then it would be too late for him to change. He was told he would have two weeks after his induction to take care of his affairs. He felt he would need those extra weeks to get ready, so he said to send his notice to him. Instead, they gave it to him and he carried it home to explain everything to me.

Our good friends from DeVilbiss High, Jean and Thad Moore, were married about the same time we were and they owned a small home near us. Thad received his draft notice in that same mailing. Thad and Harold were the first married men living in West Toledo to be drafted into the army. We invited them over to play cards with us, to talk about the draft notice and to share our feelings. We had talked on the phone earlier about taking a small trip together before the guys were drafted. We didn't play cards very long that night.

There was much discussion about where to go to get away for a few days. (This was Easter Sunday weekend.) Finally Thad said he would really like to drive to see his aunt who lived east of Ohio, right on the way to New York City. He wanted to tell her about his joining the army. Then we really got excited about going all the way to New York City. Just think, spending Easter Sunday in New York!!! (So what if the guys were not to go too far from home before their induction next Tuesday.) None of us had ever traveled that far from home.

We were very excited. Our plans were made. We decided to leave that night. They went home to pack.

19

On the way to get us, they dropped their dog inside her parent's home. We were ready when they came for us. We loaded everything in our car. (Harold had agreed to drive.) The four of us took our dog, Trixie, with us. We dropped her off in the middle of the night at my parent's house and we were on our way to New York City.

It was 3:00 A.M. on Thursday April 2, 1942 when we left Toledo. We traveled all night and into the next day. The guys took turns driving. We all had plenty of time to sleep, and we had potty stops and bought food along the way. It was great to stop driving and relax. It was fun to be with Thad and Jean. We arrived at New York City at 8:30 P.M.

Harold had called ahead to reserve two rooms for us. We were happy to see how near our hotel was to Time Square. However, our rooms were very dirty and all four of us were not very happy. Jean refused to stay there. We canceled and got reservations at a small hotel nearby. Our rooms there were perfect. We had a suite with a nice-sized living room and two bedrooms each with their own bath. It was very clean and roomy. We went out to a restaurant to eat and then walked around outside looking at the sights and the neighborhood before we returned to our rooms to sleep and get ready for a sightseeing trip in the morning. Oh how exciting it was!

When we woke up, it was Good Friday. We went shopping. We found places to eat. We went to see Banjo Eyes and the Diamond Horseshoe. The next morning we went to Chinatown and Harlem. We took a sightseeing bus. We saw the Statute of Liberty there in the Harbor.

Easter Sunday was a beautiful day. Jean and I wore our Easter Bonnets, and our Sunday clothes. Our men were all dressed up too. The hotel manager told us some places to visit and buildings to see. We spent a lot of time at Time Square. We rode the subway and took the raised train to The Bronx Zoo. We even went to see a radio broadcast studio. Harold and Thad took many pictures. Oh what a thrilling day we had!

On Monday we headed for home. We drove through the night and arrived home late on Tuesday. We stopped to visit with Thad's aunt in Pennsylvania Harold and Thad needed to be at the Induction Center early the next day. Our plan was good. Jean and Thad picked Harold up at our house and after the men were inside the Induction Center, she came back to our house to do her laundry. (Their washing machine was broken.)

Of all the housekeeping jobs, I enjoyed washing and ironing the most. My mom had a lot of shirts to iron each Monday. I always ironed the work shirts, but finally I advanced to ironing the white dress shirts. I always raced to see if I could iron shirts in a shorter time. My best time ever was 6 minutes per shirt. I always did a great job on shirts. On Tuesday morning, the clothes were ready to iron. (Dampened 'sprinkled with water' the night before and rolled tightly in a clean, dry towel.)

After lunch, we waited for the men to call, as planned, so that Jean could go get them. About 4:30 P.M. we hadn't heard from them. We had been wondering and worrying for a long time. Nobody answered the phone so Jean decided to go get them, or wait until they were finished.

When Jean returned to my house without Harold and Thad, she was very upset. They were gone! Nobody was there. The door was locked. She didn't see anyone to ask what had happened. What an awful time that was for us. We both called our mothers. We kept waiting to hear something from somebody. We didn't. I don't know if we ever ate any food.

At 6:30 we decided to go to Jean's house to do what?? Just for something to do. We were feeling sick by this time. I know we both cried a lot. Our mothers and our mothers-in-law kept calling us, again and again, to see if we heard anything. Sometime their calls kept us from really 'breaking down'. One of our mothers finally suggested that we call Western Union to see if a telegram had been sent to us. That's exactly what had happened. A telegram had been delivered to my house before 7:00 P.M. that night. I don't know who went to get the short message, hanging on my doorknob, signed by Harold and Thad. We were told that our men had been taken directly by bus to the Toledo Train Station!

He Is In The Army Now

Chapter Four

After we heard about the telegram from Harold and Thad, and we knew they had left Toledo, there was nothing more we could do. I stayed that night with Jean. I can't remember anything that happened the next day. I know that I went home that afternoon. I don't remember if I stayed alone at my house that very next day or how long it was before I heard from Harold. Jean and I each received a postcard from the Induction Center dated April 8, 1942 and postmarked from Toledo on April 9, 1942. My card said that Harold George Frutiger has been accepted for active military service. It had instructions about his transfer to Fort Benjamin Harrison where he would be for a short time and then be moved to another station. I was to wait to communicate or write to him until they sent me his proper mailing address.

I remember exactly when and how Harold came home! I was in bed at our house on Harris St. It was near morning when our doorbell rang. I looked out the bedroom window onto the front porch. It was dark outside but I could see a man in uniform standing outside our door. My first thought was, "It's Harold". I rushed to the front door, opened it up with outstretched arms. To my surprise, Thad was standing there! He said that when they arrived in Toledo, he had gone to Jean's parent's house and Harold was at my parent's place. When he knew that Jean was at his house, he turned and started to run. I'm sure he ran all the way home. Very soon Harold arrived on our porch. What a joyous reunion! Sad but very sweet! It was 6:30 A.M. on Sunday morning, April 12, 1942.

It was great to have him home again. He had a one-week pass from camp. We enjoyed being together. Most of all we talked and talked. I learned about the reason he had been taken so quickly from the Induction Center. The Army Officers were told of a Troop Train that had been sabotaged. They decided to take the newly enlisted men as quickly as possible by bus to the train station. They marched the men from the bus around the outside of the station to the train. Harold saw a man leaning against the outside wall of the station. He had written a short telegram message to me on a piece of paper he had with him on the bus. He folded some coins (money) he had in his pocket inside the note. He tossed it to that man. He watched the man catch it. All he could do was hope that I got his message telling me he was leaving for service.

Harold and Thad arrived by train at Jefferson Barracks (known by the soldiers as "Pneumonia Gulch"). They marched through pouring rain from the train to the barracks. The only clothes they had were the clothes they wore that morning. It was late that night when they arrived and Harold was assigned a lower bunk. He was not given a change of dry clothes. He went to bed and slept the night in those wet clothes. They woke him early the next morning. He was told his assignment that first day was Kitchen Police (KP). He crawled out of bed, and when the soldier sleeping in the top bunk got out of bed, Harold was very surprised. He was a classmate, a good friend from DeVilbiss High. Imagine that!

After the week at home, Harold and Thad returned to Jefferson Barracks. When Harold was waiting to be inducted into the army, friends of ours told us that a young married couple with a small child was interested in renting our house. We talked with them. We agreed on a monthly rent of $37.50. They were ready to move as soon as possible. By April 23, on Thursday, I began to think and plan to move. The day before that I was very sick and stayed with my mother all day. With the help of others, I slowly began to make some progress. My Aunt Esther and Uncle Marty bought my grandparents large farmhouse when they retired. They had two bedrooms upstairs that were empty. They offered to store our furniture.

On Sunday, April 26, we had a picnic on the farm. All the movers who came to help enjoyed that day. Harold's Aunt Edna offered to keep our refrigerator at her home in West Toledo. It replaced her icebox. She enjoyed our refrigerator until we moved it back to our home on Harris St. Our dog Trixie went to live with Harold's Aunt Marie. Trixie had a wonderful home with our aunt and uncle. She was such a smart dog. She learned easily whatever we taught her. When I had moved out of our home and the renters were beginning to move in, I went to live with my parents and my younger sister. My dad took care of collecting the rent and making our loan payments each month. What a great help that was for me. He never had any trouble collecting the rent.

Harold and Thad were soon classified at Fort Benjamin Harrison and assigned to The Army Air Force Radio School and were moved to Bellville, Illinois. Jean and I were anxious to visit them whenever we could. The first time we went to Scott Field at Belleville, near St. Louis, my dad drove his car. My mother, Harold's mother, Jean and I went with him. We stayed the first night in a hotel before we arrived at their camp. We were all very tired and needed to get some sleep. We went right to bed and woke up early the next morning to get on our way to Scott Field. Oh, the excitement of it all!

When we arrived at camp and located our 'soldiers' at their barracks, we were all very happy to see them. They were so pleased we were there. We toured the base with the guys showing us the facilities, their barracks, the mess hall, the officers quarters, etc. They had asked for and received passes for the day. We all went in Dad's car to see Belleville. It was a beautiful day. We enjoyed looking around the town, especially our time at St. Louis Zoo at Forest Park, Illinois. We hated it when we realize that it was getting time for Harold and Thad to return to their base. Soon we were on our way back to Toledo. We stayed at a small hotel for the night and woke early to finish the long drive home.

On our next two trips to Scott Field we went on the train. At each train station and bus station the local volunteers had an information center to tell visitors about the base. They had all sorts of maps, as well as a list of residents who offered their home for people to stay with them while visiting soldiers at the camp.

On both trips, Jean and I had no transportation. We asked for the nearest place so we didn't have to walk too far carrying our suitcases. The volunteers made the arrangements and gave us a map to follow. As we followed the directions, we noticed the homes were not very large and not kept up very well. We turned onto the street listed on our map. As we got closer to the house number where we were scheduled to stay, there was a very thin, much older, man outside on the sidewalk directing us to come over to him. He didn't look too good to us. He was acting weird and we were afraid. We stopped walking for a second and decided to turn around. We went back to the train station and asked for something better. Both times that we took the train to visit our husbands, we had a very good time but the days were too short and we were always dreading the time when we needed to say good bye.

Sometime during that early summer, I was hired back at Travelers Insurance. Their rules had changed and they were able to hire married women. With so many men leaving for war and women needing an income, factories were hiring women. Women were learning to do the hard jobs (men's work). Life changed for all of us!

Everybody was behind the war effort, doing good things for others. We were proud of our government, our war effort and our soldiers. The man who sold our house to us, read in the Toledo Blade (our local newspaper), that Harold had been inducted into the Army. He wrote to us that we did not need to pay any interest on our $3500.00 loan until Harold returned from service. He also wrote in that letter to contact him if we needed more help with payments.

While Harold and Thad were still in Radio School, we were eager for another chance to see them. Our plans were made and rather than take the train again, Jean wanted to drive her car and wondered if I would ride with her if she did. I said, "Sure". Her plan was to be a surprise for Thad. She wanted him to think we were arriving by train. She wasn't an experienced driver. It was a little scary when we left Toledo, but by the time we arrived at Scott Field she was driving her car like an old pro.

When we arrived at Scott Field, the Guard at the gate stopped our car. He began to ask us why we were there, whom we were visiting, and a lot of other questions. We were sure he was flirting with us (two good-looking, 21-year-old young women). He finally signaled us to enter the base. When we drove up to where Harold and Thad were standing, they were very excited and very surprised to see us with Thad's car. Thad was restricted to the base. He was being transferred to another Army Air Force School anytime that day or the next. Harold was not being transferred. He had his pass in his pocket. They had been trying to get one of their friends, (or somebody – anybody) to let Thad get into their trunk so he could get past the guard at the gate. Nobody would help in that way. They would do almost anything, but not that!

Thad was very happy to see his car on the base. That was his way out. His own trunk! Finally, in desperation, Jean agreed, and Thad got into our trunk. We closed the trunk lid. Harold walked past the guard, planning to meet us out on the highway. Jean and I arrived (with Thad in the trunk) at the Guard Post. The same guard began, again, to ask more questions. It seemed as if he was never going to signal us to go, but finally he did!

Jean (with Thad in the trunk) was shaking and trembling a lot. She could not keep her foot on the gas pedal. Our car, inch by inch, was jerking and jumping but not going forward. I put my left hand on Jean's knee so she could keep her foot on the gas. I kept holding it down, with all my strength, until we were away from that guard. She was finally able to drive. We met Harold on the highway, got Thad out of the trunk, and were on our way to our hotel rooms.

The four of us enjoyed, as best we could, the time we had together. The next day a friend of Thad phoned from camp. They were getting ready to move out. Thad should get back as soon as possible. Before we got to Scott Field, Thad was in the trunk and Harold walked into camp. A new guard was at the gate. With no problem, we drove past the guard and onto the base. We said our goodbyes. We realized it was probably the last time Harold and Thad would be stationed at the same camp and the last time that Jean and I would visit Scott Field together.

Moving To San Antonio

Chapter Five

I had a hard time getting back to normal when I came home from visiting Scott Field. I wished I could be near Harold. My job at Travelers Insurance kept me busy during the week. Harold and I sent letters to each other almost every day. It was a joy to hear from him, but I always wished I could be with him. I knew, somehow, I needed to plan, if possible, for me to follow him.

I have always enjoyed writing poems. I saved all of my poems in a stationery-sized box. Years ago I sent the best of my poems to the Toledo Blade's Poetry Contest. They returned all my poems, writing that I rhymed very well but my poems were too lengthy. One of my poems they would print if I would cut the long ending. I did! It was published. Here it is: "Is it possible to measure, the amount of pleasure, we can treasure for ever and a day, when a friendly smile is sent along its way?"

On a very gloomy day, I sat in our living room on Harris Street resting from my hard job of moving out of our house. I watched our American Flag flying above a small factory on the next street. I began to jot down a poem. This is what I wrote:

MY COUNTRY'S FLAG

My country's flag is flying high
In a troubled, grey and clouded sky.
It flutters and it waves so proud,
My spirit wants to shout aloud:
"Hurray for a symbol so strong, and sure
"Hurray for a flag that will endure."

With storm and turmoil all about,
This flag erases all my doubt.
It has a message so plain and clear.
It's there for all to see and hear.
"Rejoice in a world that is dark and grey.
"Rejoice for the clouds will roll away."

My country's flag has flown long
This promise is its faithful song:
"I will again, as in days gone by
"Fly proudly in a peaceful sky!"
Hurray for our emblem with its stripes and its stars!
Hurray for a freedom that is ever ours!

Laverne Frutiger

(Composed in 1942 at the time Laverne's husband, Harold, entered U.S. Military Services.)

This poem was printed on bulletins at flag dedications in the Toledo Ohio area.

I don't remember if I ever sent this poem to Harold when he was stationed at Scott Field. I probably didn't. I may have told him that I was attempting to write a poem about a flag as I watched it flying high in the sky from our front window. We always tried to entertain each other in our letters. He knew I was wishing and praying to be able to follow him while he was stationed in the states. I usually gave him a daily report of my activities.

In one of his letters from Scott Field, he included a postcard with a poem he wrote to me but didn't send.

Some fresh corn from Scott Field by your husband

I'm so tired

For today I eyed potatoes. I piled them 10 feet deep.
I've seen so many eyes. I'll eye them in my sleep.
On the floor, on the bench. Potatoes here. Potatoes there.
On the stove, in the pan.
Ugh, squaw work

He did tell me, before we were married, about a two-line poem he wrote in early grade school about his dog named Queenie who ate weenies.

On September 7 1942, Pvt. Harold G. Frutiger, 35325929, graduated from The Army Air Forces Technical School at Scott Field, Illinois. His letters began coming to me from San Antonio Air Cadet Corps. I knew that his hope had been to make the grade to become a pilot in the Army Air Force. I was very happy for him. He had made it to the pre-flight school.

I had been thinking and planning for the day I could move to be with him. You can only think for so long about going ahead with plans. Then you need to do something. I really wanted to be with him for his birthday on November 4. I decided to talk to my boss at Travelers Insurance about resigning before that date. He told me, among other things, that birthdays come year after year. He needed more time before I could leave the company. He agreed that I could resign in time to be with Harold for Christmas. When I got home that day, I told my family about my decision.

I planned to leave by train as soon as I could get ready after my last day of work. My family took me to the Toledo train station on the day I left for San Antonio. I stood alone on the steps of the train. I will never forget how they looked standing there at the station, as they waved 'goodbye', (especially the sad look I saw on my Dad's face from the train window as the train went by). What an ordeal that was for all of us!

I sat next to a very nice lady on the train. We talked most of the way to San Antonio. She was going home for her mother's funeral. It was a three-day trip and the train was over three hours late arriving at San Antonio. This friendly lady introduced me to her family who were there to meet her at the train station. It was getting dark and her family would not have me going alone to the rooming house where a reservation had been made for me. I rode with them to the address I had, and they waited in their car until I was safely inside the big, old house. I knew that I had missed going with the cadet wives, as planned, to visit Harold at the Army Air Force Base.

I was greeted at the door by a pleasant, motherly lady. She took me up to the third floor of the boarding house where all the cadet wives lived. They were back from their daily visit to the field. Those who had jobs near each other would, if possible, take the same bus after work to meet their husbands. They had been hoping to meet me at the field. They told me how worried Harold was when I didn't arrive with them. One wife, whose husband was a good friend of Harold at Kelly Field, had made my reservation to stay with the cadet wives at the boarding house.

I was shown which twin bed was mine. I was given one-half of one of the chest-of-drawers in the room and space in one of the closets for my clothes. There were about 10 cadet wives staying there. Our room and board was $6.50 a week. I began to unpack my belongings using the space they had shown me. The wives were very happy to see me and to talk to me. They explained the breakfast arrangement. We all ate at the large table in the living room, along with the rest of the roomers on the other floors. Our breakfast was included in our rent.

When things began to quiet down, I dressed for bed. The girls told me how to get to the downtown area the next day, and where and what time to meet them to catch the bus for Kelly Field. I was very tired and soon said 'good night'. My plan was to begin to look for a job in the morning. I fell asleep quickly now that my long trip with all my doubts and worry was over. I was so happy to be near Harold in San Antonio with a great group of cadet wives from all over the United States.

I had my first breakfast at that large boarding house table in the living room. I must have slept later than most of the renters. There were only a few men eating breakfast at the table. They looked like laborers. None of us were talking. The food was very good. The menu consisted of eggs (prepared any way I wanted them), potatoes, cereal, toast and rolls, orange juice, milk and coffee. After I ate breakfast I began my trip downtown.

I took the first job offered me. I was to report to Joske Brothers, an old-fashioned dry-goods and clothing store as soon as possible. I was hired to work in the business office.

My memory is very vague about meeting the girls to ride with them on the bus to the field. I know that when I got to the field, Harold was waiting for me. Words cannot describe how happy we were to be together. The first night I was there, we visited the Cadet Service Center. We also toured the areas around the field. Harold showed me his barracks, the Mess Hall, the class rooms, the Officers Quarters, etc. Most of the nights when I visited the field, Harold was studying hard for another quiz or test. Usually we sat on a grassy hill near his barracks, so he could study. He was trying to pass college courses. The only college classes he had were the ones he took to get his degree at Davis Business College. He had to read a lot of books. I helped him, as best I could, to review the subjects, to check his notes, and to encourage him. Neither of us knew for sure that he would get into pilot's training.

When it was time for me to leave the base, I joined the other cadet wives to catch the bus back to town. We would eat our supper at the 40-cent restaurant near our boarding house. Back at our room, we enjoyed learning about each other. All our lives were different. There were many things that we did, back home, that were the same. We talked about good and bad times we had at home before and after we married, before and after Pearl Harbor. I sent a few postcards home. I was too busy each day to think too much about home. I never told them or Harold that I hated my job at Joske Brothers.

Each cadet received, each week, one Open Post (over night pass). When the husband had an overnight pass, his wife usually arranged to rent a room at the Gunther Hotel, a beautiful hotel in downtown San Antonio.

The Cadet Club was located at the Gunther Hotel. The staff at the Cadet Club helped us in many ways. They helped us to find jobs, to get housing and they gave directions to help us get around in San Antonio. $1.50 was taken from each cadet's monthly check to pay the rent to support the Cadet Club. We stayed there whenever Harold had an over-night pass. We enjoyed meeting other cadets who were at the club enjoying the dancing and socializing. They had a juke box. We danced a lot. I cried as we danced to the new hit, "I'm Dreaming of a White Christmas" (White Christmas by Bing Crosby). Harold and I both missed, in a big way, not being home for Christmas in Toledo.

One important and emotional discussion we had back at our boarding house was our opinion of the difference between the girls from the North and those from the South. The Northern girls all felt those from the South tried to be so important: putting on airs, rolling their words, speaking softly and slowly and making us feel as if we were socially beneath them. The wives from the South were sure that the Northerners acted as if they were so important: speaking very fast and loud, pronouncing each word with such confidence, trying to keep everyone's attention. All of us were shocked! We had no idea our opinions were so negative and so different. Even today, I remember that night as a great learning point in my life. I try to better understand other people, their heritage and their opinions.

One night we talked about how our lives began to change after the bombing of our ships at Pearl Harbor. Some of us were married. Others had met the 'man' or they were working and enjoying life on their own. Some were dating interesting people. Many men were enlisting into one of the Armed Forces. Others were waiting to be drafted into the Army. Life became upsetting. One cadet wife said her happy life became like a broken egg, all mixed up with doubts, shattered plans and with a lot of worry. That expression stuck with me. Later on, I told many army wives about that discussion and feeling like Broken Eggs.

One of the cadet wives living with us on the third floor was June Marsh from Minot, N. Dakota. She was chosen to be one of three cadet wives to be featured in the April, 1943 issue of the popular magazine, Ladies Home Journal. MEET THREE ARMY AIR CORPS WIVES. We were proud to know her and we liked her. We were somewhat disappointed in the article. We felt the article was written to show the readers that our life was not easy. That it was a hard life following our men.

Quotes from Ladies Home Journal:

"Although it's an important military secret how many thousands of husky, hand-picked youngsters are training for Army Pilots within twenty miles of San Antonio, Texas, the number is plenty to explain why San Antonio so teems with girls wearing tiny pins in the shape of wings….

"San Antonio's girl-flood situation worries the Air Corps. The close proximity of a lonesome young wife can be even more of a psychological handicap to the a cadet under the heavy strains of pilot training than if she were merely writing mournful letters from West Virginia. It also worries San Antonio, which has to cope with problems of living quarters and employment for cadet wives….

"…..all she has to look forward to after her nightly hour at the base, is a solitary forty-cent supper at one of the fantastically crowded and utterly don't-care restaurants…" (A few comments from the article about cadet wives in the Ladies Home Journal)

Most of us were satisfied with the life that we or our husband chose for us.

We felt we were doing a pretty good job of keeping our husbands happy. We felt we were keeping our marriage stable and secure.

Every nine weeks the Air Force Cadets finished their courses and were moved to another base, sometimes quite a distance from San Antonio. About two weeks before Christmas, Harold took his test for Pilot's School. He passed the test! What a relief that was! He would now be actually flying airplanes. Rumors were that he was going to Chickasha, Oklahoma.

Chickasha, Oklahoma

Chapter Six

A few days after Harold's graduation, we were on our way to the Flight School at Chickasha, Oklahoma. He found out at the base that the almost-for-sure rumors were a safe bet and he wanted me to get to Chickasha as soon as possible. I told the cadet wives, my landlady at the boarding-house, and my boss at Joske Brothers that I would be moving. I packed my belongings and left my friends and my life there with mixed emotions. However, I felt that the time I spent at San Antonio had been exciting and I looked forward to my new adventure.

On my way to Chickasha, I began to relax. I learned that a young lady sitting more to the back was going to Chickasha, too. I went to talk to her. She was on her way to join her husband at the flight training school also. Her home was in Cleveland, Ohio, not too far from my home back east in Toledo, Ohio. We spent most of the time on the trip sitting together, getting to know each other. Her name was Agnes Pollock. By the time we arrived at our destination we were good friends and we stayed with each other as we gathered our luggage and began our life together in Chickasha, Oklahoma.

Chickasha was a very small town. We could walk from one end of the town to the other. The downtown was very old and quaint. The shops were small and most of them were on the main street. There were benches where shoppers sat to visit or to rest before going to another store or to the bank or the post office, etc.

Agnes and I looked around the town for a short time. When we saw a Welcome Center office, we went inside to talk to someone. We were anxious to ask about lodging and also available jobs. We were told about a nice elderly couple living close to town who had a small apartment upstairs in their home for rent. They said they only rented to small families of army personnel and that we could walk there from town. Also, I was told of a secretarial position at the government school located about a quarter of a mile outside of Chickasha. They called ahead and arranged for us to see the little apartment, and also made an appointment for me to talk to the director of the school that afternoon. We left our luggage at the Welcoming Center and walked to the rental apartment.

When we reached the little home with the cute brick porch on the front, we rang the door bell. An elderly man and his wife opened the door to greet us. We liked them right from the start. They encouraged us to come in and they began to tell us about the small apartment they made in their upstairs area. The stairway to the upstairs was across the foyer at the front door. We noticed immediately that we would not need to enter any part of their living quarters as we went up to the apartment. The door to the apartment was at the top of the stairs. As we entered, we both knew it was perfect for us. There was a nicely furnished small living room inside the door. It had a bay of windows at the far end of the room. To the left they had turned a small closet into a kitchen with a breakfast bar with two chairs for us to sit on to eat. A sink, stove and refrigerator were built at the very end of the closet. The only bedroom was at the right of the kitchen. We were happy with the arrangements and with the price.

On the way downstairs, they told us about the guest room on the first floor near the front door. We could rent that room by the night whenever we needed it. This was perfect for us! We paid the rent and hurried back to get our luggage. As we walked into town, we were very happy that we had found such a cute place. However, we both felt the couple looked somewhat sad at various times during our visit.

It was near to lunch time, so we ate at a small restaurant before we returned to our apartment with our luggage. My appointment at the government school was in the afternoon. As soon as we dropped our things off at the apartment, I wanted to stay there and enjoy our new place but I needed to hurry to get to my interview.

As I walked through the farm field to get to the new government school building, I was feeling very pleased with how well the morning had gone. The woman secretary there interviewed me. She told me they needed one person to help her in the office. The students were mostly of Indian background, 1/2 Indian, full Indian, 1/4 Indian, etc. I learned they were mostly young boys, 16 years old or older, enrolled in that school. The instructors at the school taught the students how to do skilled labor such as welding, woodworking, carpentry, auto repairing, etc. Many lived at the school. They ate their meals there and the food was good. When the boys finished their training, they were taken to work in government factories in the big cities.

I was hired on the spot and was instructed to report for work as soon as I could get settled into my apartment. I liked the lady who interviewed me. I would be working with her in the office. My pay was great and I could eat my lunch every day at the cafeteria. I was "on cloud nine" as I walked 'home' thinking about our apartment and my new job! When I arrived at our apartment, it was getting time for Agnes and I to get ready to go to the train station before the troop train arrived from San Antonio. We had been told earlier that a train was due about 7:00 P.M. If it was the troop train, we didn't want to miss it. We decided to get down to the train station as early as possible. The small station was very near to the town of Chickasha and it didn't take us long to walk there.

There were four or five other young women waiting there, sitting in the uncomfortable seats. We learned they were cadet wives waiting for that same train. We had all traveled some distance and were really too tired to be very talkative. We mostly just sat there, with our own private thoughts, waiting for that troop train to arrive, and hoping our men would be on it.

There was a quiet little man sitting behind the glass window separating his office from the visitor's seats. He kept his visor cap on and worked at papers at his desk. He looked at us, from time to time, with a rather sad and disappointing look. After a while, I asked him if I could borrow a sheet of paper. He was happy to give me a sheet and a pencil. I had the address of our apartment and the telephone number of the place we had rented. Our landlord had told us that we could receive phone calls there at any time. I quickly wrote a note for Harold, hoping I would see him as he departed from the train to tell him of our nice apartment, my job at the Government School and to give him a phone number where he could reach me at the apartment. I was anxious to tell him about my first day in Chickasha.

We sat, for what seemed forever, waiting for that troop train to arrive. The little man kept watching us and finally came over to talk to us. It was approaching 11:00 P.M. He told us he was not allowed to tell us about the arrival of "our" train but if we would go home now, say nothing to anybody, and be back by 7:00 A.M. we would not miss anything. He told us he didn't like to see us waiting there all night. I thank that sweet little man to this day for that kindness.

We cadet wives returned in the morning and waited. I was hoping that the troop train would arrive and that Harold would be on that train. It wasn't too long before a train pulled into the station. We waited breathlessly for the doors to open and the passengers to begin to exit. Finally they started coming slowly at first and then a lot quicker. It was evident that they had been sleeping through the night and they were trying to wake up and make themselves and their wrinkled uniforms presentable. Finally, I saw Harold and I ran over to embrace him. We were so happy to be together. I had just enough time to give him the note I had written for him. The line of soldiers kept coming off the train and he needed to move on. I knew that he would contact me as soon as he had an opportunity to call.

Agnes and I loved our apartment. We enjoyed being there whenever we could. Agnes never found a job in Chickasha. Oklahoma City was a long bus ride away. She decided not to go there to look for work. She was happy to stay near her husband to spend more time with him. I went to work at the government school on Monday and every day after that was exciting and different. While I was working at the school, Government Officials came to meet with all our school employees. We were expected to be there for each of their two-hour sessions. Their main endeavor was to teach us 'How To Teach'. The one thing I still remember from their seminar was the phrase the instructors said over and over: "If the pupil hasn't learned, the teacher hasn't taught". In addition to our learning how to teach, we also learned how to keep good records in the office and advice for the instructors to keep good records also. They had rules we all needed to learn about how to keep the cafeteria food pure and tasty, and the kitchen and dining hall clean.

Harold called me in a very short time after he arrived at the flight school, and he was very happy that I was so happy with my work and my apartment. I would take the bus to the air field to be with him as often as possible. We would spend our time at the pilot's Cadet Club on the base. We held hands a lot. He was very happy there. He was learning a lot and was very pleased with his grades. He and Agnes' husband, Frank, did not get many passes to leave the base. Harold sent a few postcards home to our parents and I tried to write a letter to them often.

It was getting close to Christmas, our first Christmas away from home! The little town of Chickasha, Oklahoma was all decorated for the season and I was busy shopping after work and on Saturday for Christmas gifts for everybody back home. I was happy to buy Christmas wrapping paper, ribbons and tape. I was most concerned about buying something very special for Harold. He badly needed a new wrist watch band. I went to every jewelry store and every jewelry department. I finally found the band I wanted and I was so happy when I purchased that gold band for him. It didn't cost too much and I had the money to buy it. When I came home from shopping, I showed Agnes many of my purchases. I showed her my treasured wrist watch band.

When Harold was able to get a one day pass, we spent a lot of the day at our apartment, showing each other the gifts we each bought to send home for Christmas. Together we wrapped them and packed a box for his family and another box for my family. I sent them to Toledo in plenty of time for Christmas. We received a very large package from our families and I stored it in our living room near the Christmas tree, waiting to open it on Christmas Eve. Our landlords where happy that Agnes and I were pleased with the Christmas tree they put up for us.

Our husbands both had weekend passes for Christmas Eve and Christmas Day. The Pollocks were planning to go to Midnight Mass so they had their gift exchange while Harold and I went to an early service at the Lutheran Church nearby. When we returned from church, Agnes and Frank were already out of the apartment. We were anxious to get at opening our gifts. One of the first gifts we opened from Toledo was a framed photo of my Mom and Dad taken at our church in Toledo by a professional photographer. I was very homesick and I could not keep from crying. I knew that Harold was homesick too. We continued to open the rest of our presents and we enjoyed receiving each and every gift. I was very happy when Harold opened his present from me. He was so pleased to see that beautiful wrist watch band.

When it was time for the Pollocks to return from church, we cleaned up our Christmas mess. We took our gifts downstairs to the guest bedroom with the feeling that we survived our first Christmas away from home and that we were so happy to have each other. The next morning, when we got together with Agnes and Frank around the Christmas tree in our apartment, we were all very happy we had met each other and were great friends. That was until Frank showed us his beautiful wrist band he received from Agnes. It was the exact watch band I had bought for Harold! She never mentioned to me that she had decided to buy a watch band for Frank just like the one I had for Harold.

It wasn't too long after that, we learned the Cadet pilot who rented the apartment just before we moved in had been killed in an accident while flying at the air base. No wonder the elderly couple sometimes seemed so sad. After Christmas the cadets were back at the base studying hard for classes and tests they needed to pass. The weather had been bad and it was about two weeks until they could get up in the air to fly. Harold had received a note from my Dad telling him how pleased he was that he was doing so well at Pilot School. I continued to go out to the field whenever I could.

Finally the weather turned good and Harold and his instructor went up to continue flying lessons. When I came to the field that evening Harold was looking awful. He could hardly say anything to me. I knew something was wrong. He had a hard time telling me that he had been "washed out" of Pilot's Training that day. We sat there, holding hands, but not being able to say anything. Harold couldn't talk about it and I didn't know what to say! For both of us it became one of the saddest days of our life together. I learned from somebody that night that orders came from Headquarters to eliminate a large group of cadets from the class immediately. No one seemed to know why!

Much later Harold was able to talk about it and to tell me, in detail, what happened that day. He said his instructor was not the most pleasant teacher. He was going through a divorce and was mean and irritated a lot of the time. Harold's task that day was to put the airplane into a deep dive and pull out of it successfully. His dive was deeper than it should have been. When he pulled out of the dive quickly and successfully, he looked over and realized his instructor had fainted! Harold flew without his instructor's help until he had landed the airplane on the ground and taxied into the hangar. When the plane had stopped and the instructor got out of the cockpit and entered the hangar, he turned around and said in just a few words that for Harold it was over. He was "Washed Out". He was one of The Chickasha Class Of 43-F to be sent back to be reclassified. Within a few days, we were on our way back to San Antonio. We had to leave that good life in Chickasha. We had to say goodbye to our happiest days and our saddest days!

Our wedding day, June 7, 1941.

With our wedding attendants at Augsburg
Lutheran Church.

On our honeymoon June 1941

Honeymoon in Canada

Our car on our honeymoon

Honeymoon

Honeymoon in Canada

Honeymoon in Canada

Harold in our driveway on Harris Street

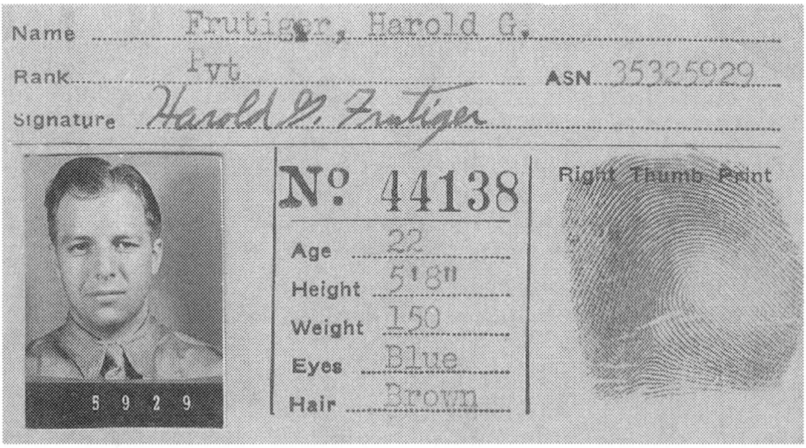

Name Frutiger, Harold G.

Rank Pvt ASN 35325929

Signature Harold G. Frutiger

No 44138

Age 22

Height 5'8"

Weight 150

Eyes Blue

Hair Brown

Right Thumb Print

Identification card

TOLEDO, OHIO (Induction station) APR 8 - 1942 (Date)

This is to advise you that

Harold George Frutiger, (Name) (Army Serial No. if accepted) has been

~~*rejected for active military service and returned to his home.~~

*accepted for active military service. He has left this station en route to a reception center at FT.BENJ.HARR.,IND.REC.CENTER where he will remain for a short time and then be sent to another station. As he will be in transit for the next few days, it will be difficult for mail to reach him. It is therefore requested that no attempt be made to communicate with him except in an emergency until you receive further advice as to the address to which mail for him should be sent.

This card to be made out and mailed at induction station at time of transfer therefrom.

*Strike out clause not applicable.

W. D., A. G. O. Form No. 202
October 1, 1941 16—18394-1 U. S. GOVERNMENT PRINTING OFFICE

Postcard sent to me on April 8, 1942

Cartoon from 1942

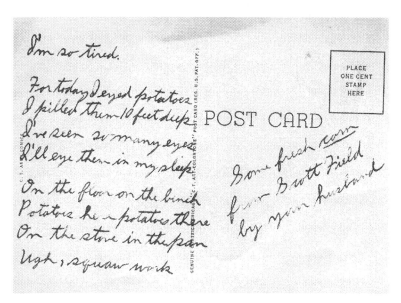

Postcard with poem written by Harold at Scott Field

Harold and I with Agnes Pollock, S. 7th St., Chickasha, OK
Jan. 12, 1943

Aviation Cadet

"Into the Wild Blue Yonder"

Open post at Classification Center.
Just leaving for a day in San Antonio.

Guard Duty at Classification Center

Harold with his dad, Rudy, and his brother, Ken

Home at the farm in Temperance, MI

Harold and his father-in-law, Art Welling

Shopping with Harold

At my parent's home with my sister, Evelyn, and "Susie".

Houston, TX   March 7, 1943

Celebrating Jean and Victor Meeker's wedding,
March 27, 1943, Houston, TX

Big Spring Herald, Big Spring, Texas, Thursday, May 6, 1943

Meet The Bombardiers

Musicians, Athletes Among Cadets

There are musicians and athletes and hobbyists of many another shade—in the new class of cadets in training at the Big Spring Bombardier School. Introducing others of the group:

OHIO

An industrial chemical salesman from Toledo is Harold Frutiger. He's a product of DeVilbiss high school and the Davis business college, and his hobby is anything musical. He's played in dance bands for five years, and actually had his own band for two years. Then from Middleton we have Mack Long, a junior clerk in the accounting department of the Republic Steel

He's a Gamma Sigma, and he played varsity football and baseball both in high school and college. Bob couldn't wait to finish college. He left to join the army last July. He'd like to wind up as an athletic coach after the war.

PENNSYLVANIA

There are thirteen boys from the Keystone state. Johnny Gides comes from Lilly. He's a coal miner who goes for baseball and photography. Joe Grimm is a Pittsburgh boy. He spent several years at the University of Pittsburgh, and then got himself a job as a complaint clerk. His hobbies are music and dramatics which must come often in very handy when

is an office clerk from the Quaker City. Francis Xavier Pierce is the name, and his last job was with the Breyer's Ice Cream company. Francis' ambition in life is to get married.

RHODE ISLAND

Frank Dominic Pinto comes from Providence. He's a product of Rhode Island State college and Providence college, and earned his living as a radio repairman and a furniture serviceman up to 1937 when he joined the army. His special talent is playing the violin, and he's had some experience playing in dance bands. Frank's brother, Ray, is in the army, and

Newspaper clipping from the Big Spring Herald,
Thursday, May 6, 1943

Harold with me in my maternity dress, Big Spring, TX

Army Air Forces Bombardier School

of

Big Spring, Texas

announces the graduation of

Class 43-10

Thursday, the fifteenth day of July

Nineteen hundred forty-three

Post Theatre

Announcement of Harold's graduation from
Bombardier School

Graduation from Army Air Forces Bombardier School,
Big Spring, TX

Our mailbox on the ranch we rented in Big Spring.

With Mildred Futrell in Big Spring, TX

Home in Big Spring, TX with Sharon Kay

The Frutiger family, Big Spring, TX

Lieutenant Harold G. Frutiger

Back To San Antonio

Chapter Seven

Within a few days we headed back to San Antonio, Texas. We both left Chickasha, Oklahoma with sad hearts. Harold went on the troop train with the loss of a dream for which he had worked so hard to earn. My loss seemed great too. I loved my life there. When I arrived at San Antonio, I went directly to the Cadet Center. I needed a place to stay and a list of office jobs available. They said rooms and apartments for rent were scarce. They told me about a very respectable lady who, each week, rented a room for one or two nights on Saturday and Sunday only. They also advised me to go for an interview at a large new department store. The store was hiring several people to work that weekend only.

For a more permanent place to live, they told me about a young married couple with a five-year old boy. They rented their extra bedroom which had a room with two twin beds. The volunteer phoned ahead to have one bed reserved for me until I got there. The other twin bed was being held for the wife of another service man. I decided to go to get the typing job first. I left my luggage behind. After I was hired, I went on a bus to find the room available to be shared by two army wives. The family was very nice and their little boy was cute. They would provide food with the room if I wanted to do that. I did. We settled for a weekly rate and I told them I would be back with my luggage.

I was hoping that the room for the weekend would be OK. I needed to take a bus there. A very pleasant lady greeted me at the door. She lived in a very nice house in an elegant neighborhood and I was very pleased. I talked with her for quite a while. I was hoping maybe I could live there all the time Harold and I were in San Antonio. I decided not to mention it at that time. (The room might not be very satisfactory.) I went back to the Cadet Center to gather my belongings and to thank the ladies for all their help. I told them I was pleased with everything.

When I arrived back at the room where I would be staying for the next two nights, I was very tired. It had been a long Friday and since I had eaten at a restaurant on my way downtown, I was ready for bed. That night the landlady invited me to sit with her in the family room. She had a quart jar filled with shelled pecans grown on a tree in her yard. It was the only time I had ever eaten tasty pecans from the jar until I was full. And then I ate some more. The lady and I talked about a lot of things. She told me that her husband had a drinking problem and that he was gone with friends, men and women, every weekend. She told me that her weekends were very lonely. I felt sorry for her. I told her some things about my life in Ohio and my life, so far, following my husband. After a while, I told her how much I had enjoyed being with her, and said goodnight. I took a long, hot bath and went to bed. I needed to get up early in the morning to go to my job at the department store. I gave thanks for how well things had worked for me that day.

When I went to the typing job the next morning, I was escorted to a large room with many desks, each with a typewriter. They showed me where I should sit. They gave me some instructions and a lot of papers to copy. I was left there with the other typists and some new people came in to work and were given the same instructions. It was easy for me and I was enjoying the job a lot. Suddenly I became aware of the girl typing next to me. She was not a good typist. She was struggling with her typewriter, using the hunt and poke system. I felt sorry for her. I could not stop typing to help her. I felt she was an army wife and needed the job, any job, to continue living near her husband.

There were store employees watching us as we worked. They did not talk to the girl typing next to me about her work. She kept trying to do her best. I was happy for her. I had met a lot of army wives struggling to have enough money to follow their husband. When we went to be paid as planned, we all received double-time for the hours we worked. A lady in the employment office called for me to come to her desk. She asked if I could come back on Monday for a more permanent job. When I said "yes," she told me to come to the top floor on Monday. Someone would meet me at the president's office and explain more about the work. "Wow!" I went back to my rented room on 'cloud nine'!

When I rang the doorbell, the lady opened the door with a big smile. She was happy to see me. I told her about my day. As I went up to my room, she called to invite me to come down, if I wanted to, and we could talk a while. When I was somewhat relaxed, I did just that and we again had a good time talking. We ate more of the shelled pecans she poured out from that quart jar. This, too, had turned out to be a wonderful day for me. In the morning I slept in. After a long, long sleep and when I was fully awake, I started to think more about Harold and how much I wanted to tell him all that had happened to me.

I don't remember when I was able to reach Harold at the classification center. I know that I was able to talk to him on the phone shortly after he arrived in San Antonio. I briefly told him about my work at the department store and the telephone number and address where I would be living. He was very happy to hear about my more permanent job at the department store.

After I packed my suitcases and said goodbye to my nice landlord, I walked to the bus line to go to my next adventure! When I arrived at the small, neat little house, I immediately felt right at home. Their little boy was a cute kid. My roommate was there and she seemed very pleasant. I learned, as we talked, that she was from New Jersey, of Jewish background. We liked each other right from the start. We talked about a lot of things that night. The next morning, I left early to get to my job on time. I went upstairs to the president's office. There was a folding card table and a folding card table chair set up outside the president's office. A secretary there gave me plenty of work to do and I found out early on that they liked my work. As the days went on, I developed a sore back. I didn't want to complain, so I said nothing about my hurting backache. I didn't ask for a better chair.

Harold wasn't getting any leave time, but I was really too tired to try to find the bus to his air base. By the time we had our evening supper and sat in the living room to talk and to listen to the radio, I was ready for bed.

My roommate and I talked into the night. I was always happy to talk on the phone with Harold whenever he called me, for as long as he could stay on the telephone line.

Before the first weekend came, I received a call from Harold's Aunt Marie. It was good to hear from her. She and Uncle Walter and their daughter, Dorothy, were driving to Texas to visit Dorothy's husband stationed near San Antonio at Austin, Texas. They wanted to plan a time to visit with us. I became very excited. She gave me the telephone number where they would be staying. I called Harold and he was very eager to get a pass to spend the day with us. This was the first time anyone from our family had come to see us. Harold did get a day pass and I arranged to have them meet me at the house where I lived. I became very excited as it came closer to the time for them to arrive. I cried with happiness as they came from their car to greet me.

First we went to the base to get Harold. It was so good to be with him. He was very happy to see us. Together with 'our family' we went to look around his quarter (his barracks, the mess hall, and all the other buildings). We met some of his friends there. Then we decided to tour San Antonio. It was a great day for all of us. The weather was beautiful.

We visited the famous Alamo. Our guide explained the battle and the history. We enjoyed hearing the reason for the Alamo's fame. We learned that it was an old Spanish Mission, built in 1718. When the friars abandoned the mission, Spanish soldiers soon occupied the Alamo. When Texas decided to separate from Mexico, Texan soldiers fought against the Mexicans who occupied The Alamo. In December, 1835, Texas took control of San Antonio and the Alamo. That siege lasted for 13 days with only about 15 fighters still alive when that part of the war was over. William Travis and a slave, Joe, survived. In 1836, Texas became an independent nation.

Other soldiers continued the ongoing fight against Mexico. Stephen Austin, from Virginia, came to fight in the war for Texas. Some other men who fought in that war were James Bowie, Davy Crockett and Sam Houston. Finally they defeated Mexico and Sam Houston became the first President of the Republic of Texas. On December 29, 1845, Texas joined the United States as the 28th state. We learned that Texas is the only state in the USA to have been an independent nation. Aunt Marie, Uncle Walter, Dorothy, Harold and I were all very impressed with the guide and the information that was available for us.

The San Antonio Zoo was next on our list to visit. We decided we did not have enough time to visit the zoo. We had heard about Brackenridge Park which was located near the zoo. We went there and had a very enjoyable trip through the gardens with all the flowers, the beautiful shrubs, the ornate stone bridges and walkways up and down the park. Uncle Walter took many movies of the beauty around us. We knew it was getting time for us to get Harold back to his base and for our relatives to head back to Austin, Texas.

When they dropped me off at my home, I wished I had more time to be with them. I was tired and after I said goodbye and they drove away, I was more than ready to 'call it a day'. What a happy day it was! I relaxed and had time to listen to the radio, and to talk to my adopted family and my roommate, before I went to my room to get ready for bed and for my job in the morning.

Every night, after my roommate and I ate our supper and helped in the kitchen, we listened to the radio in their small living room. We enjoyed the sit-coms, Fibber McGee and Molly, George Burns and Gracie Allen, The Lone Ranger and his Horse, Silver, The Green Hornet, and the scary radio show, The Shadow. We listened carefully to the news announcements and we always had the President on when he had his Fireside Chats, his New Deal, and his often mentioned, "My Friends."

The people I lived with loved our President, Franklin D. Roosevelt. They were vocal and thrilled with everything he said. I listened but never said anything. I made as few comments as I could think of that were appropriate. I'm a dedicated Republican, always was and always will be. I believe in a smaller government, lower taxes and less money spent by a bigger and bigger government. I always worked for and voted in the Primary Elections and the National Elections, for the people I believed were the best running for election in my party. I encouraged everyone to study the causes and speeches of candidates of the Democrats, the Republicans, and the Independents, and to vote for the person they thought was best. I believe in free speech and the right for all Americans to register to vote.

When we two wives went to our room after listening to the President's speech that first night, we began to talk about what the president had said. We were amazed that neither one of us liked our President. We didn't say too much about FDR and we never discussed him again. He was our President and we honored him. We sat silently the next time our president had his Fireside Chat, as we listened to him on the radio.

The little boy in our house was always happy to sit with us in the living room after supper. We had fun playing with him until he went to bed. He was a smart boy and his parents gave him a lot of their attention. He seemed to have a lot of nervous tension and sometimes had an upset stomach. It seemed that he needed cola syrup quite often for him to settle down for bed. At times one of his parents needed to hurry to the drug store before it closed to get more cola syrup for him. I wasn't around to see much of their parenting during the day. I didn't learn about parenting until we had our first baby. Later, when we had our first baby, I found it's terrible to be a parent of a first child, especially if you are away from your family and/or other parents.

My job in that beautiful department store was a very nice job. I was happy to work there. When I came home from work, and my roommate and I were in our room for the night, she massaged my aching back to relax it. That helped me to feel a lot better. I slept late on the weekends and mostly spent time to read and to relax. I never looked for a church to visit in San Antonio. I really didn't want go to church alone. Harold did not have much spare time at the base. His days there were long and he felt he needed to relax too. It wasn't too long before he called me, telling me he was shipping out soon. I needed to get to Houston, Texas.

The next day I told my boss at work that I was moving to Houston, Texas as soon as possible. She said I could leave the next day. Since a lot of their employees were army wives, they were prepared for us to leave on a day's notice. When I went to receive my final pay check, the person helping me with the forms that I needed to fill out, noticed that I had been paid double time all the while I worked for them. Everyone got very excited. My pay should have been changed to regular time after that first day I worked for them on that weekend. I sat quietly while they figured out what they could do about the problem. They finally gave me a check for double time, wished me well in Houston and thanked me for my work with them. How about that! Again, I hated to leave San Antonio. It was hard to say goodbye, but after I packed my bags and headed for the bus station, I was anxious to be on my way to Houston, Texas.

Houston, Texas

Chapter Eight

The day I left San Antonio on that bus to Houston, Texas I was not really ready to go. Harold was reassigned quicker than I planned. I didn't want to leave the family I was living with. I liked being part of that very nice family. I didn't have anybody to travel with and I felt for some reason alone. I wasn't sure what Harold's duties would be at the air field. Plus, it was hard to say goodbye.

When my bus pulled into Houston, I was surprised to see such a small, clean, and modern downtown area. It was not a big city. There were some small high-rise buildings with not much more than eight stories in each building. As the bus pulled into town, I began to remember my home town, Toledo, Ohio's downtown area. Toledo was much larger than Houston and very dirty. Toledo and Detroit, Michigan were auto manufacturing towns and I remembered all the soot on everything. Thinking about home, while sitting on that bus, made me feel homesick for Toledo.

As soon as I left the bus with my luggage, I began to search for the Hospitality Center. When I found it, I relaxed and enjoyed the company of the volunteers working there. They told me of a nice home in a nice neighborhood. Two single ladies had a very lovely room they rented to a wife of a serviceman and I was assured I would be pleased to live there. I had the directions to get there by bus, and with the street address, I started on my way.

When that bus stopped for me and I went up the steps, I looked around and I began to worry. All the seats were filled except for the first front seat on either side of the aisle facing the front and the two seats ahead of them, one on each side of the bus facing each other. Behind these empty seats, the aisle was filled with people standing. It looked like all the people on the bus were black people. I put my coins into the money receiver and sat on the first seat on the left side facing the front. At the next stop, soon after I sat down, a black man entered the crowded bus and after he paid his coins, he sat in front of me on the bench facing the center of the bus. As the bus started and we were going along, the driver began to yell at the black man for sitting down in front of a white lady. When the man stood up and hung onto one of the straps in front me, the bus driver was terribly angry. He yelled at the man, telling him to "get to the back". The man moved immediately to the back of the crowded bus. I felt very sorry for that black man.

Everyone was quiet on the bus. I noticed that we had left the more crowded and busy neighborhood. The homes were farther apart and the area was much nicer. Soon the bus driver pulled up to a stop and parked the bus at the curb in front of a drugstore situated with a few other stores at that corner. He took his money changer from the holder and carried it with him, down the steps and through the open bus door. I watched the door close behind the bus driver and saw him enter the drugstore. I felt so alone. I did not notice any other white people on the bus. I came the point of being in a state of panic. I tried to shrink down into my seat, to be as small as possible. I did not look to the right or to the left.

Talking began softly behind me. Finally the voices became louder and more violent with fists flying behind me and nasty oaths being yelled out from those angry people. I too, was very angry at the bus driver. I was saying over and over, under my breath, "Oh Lord, please help me. Please help me!" It seemed to me it was a long time after the driver left until he returned. In my mind, I felt the bus driver took time to drink a cup of coffee after he had been to the bathroom in the drugstore. When the bus driver finally returned, as he stepped onto the bus, extreme quiet returned immediately. It took a while for me to breathe normally again. I learned later that it was Friday morning and all the people on that bus were going to work as hired help in the wealthy neighborhood, or they were there to see about getting an advertised job at one of those elegant homes. As the people gradually left the bus and I watched for my stop, I began to relax. I never told anybody, not even Harold, about my bus ride on that first day I was in Houston. I didn't want to add gossip to the problems the black people already had.

My room was on the first floor of a ranch-type home. It was a beautiful and very large room. It had a frilly, all-white bedspread and pillows, with a dressing table with matching white frilly full skirt and a cute chair with lace to match the white skirt. There were many windows in the room that let in plenty of light, overlooking a well cared-for lawn. The two owners were very attractive people much older than I was. Both of them were divorcees with good jobs in Houston. Most weekends they went for an overnight visit to Galveston, a nearby town in Texas. Sometimes they drove by themselves and other times a very nice man, a long time friend about their age, came to pick them up in his car. He dropped over sometimes during the week and I enjoyed his company when he was there. My landlords told me that on the weekends, Harold could stay with me, whenever he had an overnight pass.

On Monday, the first day I was there, I went looking for a job. I learned from the Welcome Center about some jobs that were available. I was hired soon by the Knutson Construction Company. They had built at least two huge warships for the army while their business was located in Houston, Texas. They had occupied the top two floors of a new 8-story high-rise building. But now they were moving out of Houston and only three men remained there to settle up their business move. They didn't have much to do, so it was a very easy job for them and for me. I was the only secretary and I was able to keep up with all the work they had for me to do.

I contacted Harold as soon as I was able to get a telephone number for him. He told me how to get to Ellington Field from downtown. All wives were allowed to visit the field at certain hours every day. The only place we could meet our husbands was at the chapel. The rule was that nobody would be turned away from the chapel during visiting hours. The bus would drop us off at the chapel and return again when it was time for us to leave the base. I went on the bus every night after work. The bus to Ellington Field was always filled with wives going to be with their husbands. We went to all the different religious services scheduled for each week. All of us, men and women, liked the Jewish services the best.

The servicemen who belonged to that church explained that their faith carried on the old tradition of the church service being a meeting place for friends and family, and that we could move around to greet other friends and could talk with each other during the service. We talked quietly and never felt like we were disturbing others. We were able to tell our mates about our week while we were away from each other.

When the services were over and we were waiting outside for the bus to come, we hugged and kissed our mates goodbye. We were always happy when the bus was late. There came a time, while I was there, that Ellington Field posted a rule that there would be no showing of affection outside the church. We felt that holding hands was OK and we were able to tell our mates how much we missed them when we were not together.

I really liked my work during the week. My bosses were fun to work for. They teased me a lot. There were days when they would be away from the office for long periods of time. I was alone in the office a lot. This turned out to be a blessing for me. I had been working there for about a month. We were into March of 1943 and Lent was being celebrated already. Easter Sunday was approaching and I was very happy with my life in Houston.

About that time, I began to feel very ill, sick to my stomach every morning.

I didn't realize for a while that I was pregnant. Even when I felt I knew I was, I didn't want to talk about it to anybody. I wanted to tell Harold before I told anybody else.

At work I was very happy that I had an easy job and that I didn't have much work to do each day. My paycheck was $37.50 per week which seemed like a fortune to me. My desk was in the outer office. My bosses each had an office connected to the outer office. Our coat closet was next to the outer office. The ladies restroom was directly across the hall from our offices. That was perfect for me. I had not been to a doctor since I arrived in San Antonio in November, 1942. I did not plan to see a doctor until after I went with Harold to our next station. I told Harold, as soon as I was certain, that we were expecting a baby. Both of us were happy about our coming event.

On my way home from Ellington Field, I realized that one of the wives from the field lived just a few houses from where I was boarding. We became friends and when we returned from our nightly visit with our men at the field, we spent some time talking and laughing together at one of our rooms. Her place was more of a rooming house with several upstairs bedrooms rented by young people. I really liked to be at her place because there was a sofa in a small living room at the top of the stairs and other roomers would join us just to talk.

One day I received a letter from a girl friend who worked with me at Travelers Insurance in Toledo, Ohio. It was good to hear from somebody in addition to our family letters from home. Jean Collins' letter was exciting. She wrote that her boyfriend from West Toledo was stationed at Ellington Field and he wanted her to come to Houston to be married! I answered by return mail that I was very happy living near Harold and I knew she would be happy too. I knew Victor Meeker. His sister worked with Jean and me at the insurance Company in Toledo.

Harold and Vic got together and made the wedding plans. The cadet wife living near me told me about a room for rent on their second floor. We put a hold on it and we had a perfect place for Jean to live. Our plans were working out just fine. My boss found a hotel room for the bride and groom. The chapel at Ellington

Field was ready with flowers and the Army Chaplain performed the wedding ceremony. Harold and I were their attendants. They were married on March 27, 1943. The four of us went out to dinner after the wedding. We had a wonderful time toasting the bride and groom. We were happy that they were married. All of us knew that the right thing had been done and we were thrilled that everything worked out so well.

The next day our husbands returned to the field and Jean moved in the boarding house near to me. Usually she took the bus to Ellington Field earlier than I did. We joined them at the chapel and Jean and I and our friend who roomed with Jean took the bus home together after the church service. It was a good life for us. On Easter Sunday, 1943, we three couples planned to spend some of the day at a beautiful park in Houston and then travel by bus to Galveston to spend some time at the beach. Harold and I arranged with Frank and Agnes Pollock, who shared our apartment in Chickasha, Oklahoma, to meet us at the park. They were stationed at Ellington Field and we saw them occasionally. We four couples had a relaxing afternoon, so relaxed that we decided not to go to Galveston. Later in the day, we took a bus downtown to spend time looking around the town of Houston.

About that time, my mother sent me an article clipped from our Toledo, Blade: "NINE OF AREA TRAIN AT ELLINGTON FIELD" "Eight Toledoans and one Holland, Ohio, man, are training as bombardiers and navigators at the Army Air force training school at Ellington Field, Tex." The item listed one of the Bombardiers as Harold G. Frutiger, 4202 Harris St. A future Navigator is Victor K. Meeker, 1609 Homestead Street.

It was getting near to when the Cadets would be graduating from the training school. We were already concerned about when our next orders would be final. About that time, as we sat in the small family room one evening, one of the wives, whose husband was in the Army overseas and we had learned to know her and to enjoy her company, came to talk with us. After a short time she began to cry. She sobbed a lot! She told us that the young man, boarding in the room next to her, had spent time with her and now she was pregnant with his child. She did not want the child, she was afraid to tell her husband and she didn't know what to do.

This news shocked all of us! We felt terrible for the girl. It became our worry immediately. What was she to do? What could we do for her? The next evening, all the abortion ideas we had heard about were being put forward. The girl was willing to try any of them, all of them! Some of the girls were walking her backward up and down the stairs. Others were in the kitchen, making a concoction for her to drink. About two or three days later, Harold's orders came for him to ship out to Big Spring, Texas. I began to pack up to follow him. I had the feeling I was forgetting something but I covered all bases. Everything in my room was packed and when I knew nothing of mine was left behind, I headed for the bus. I never heard the rest of the story about that sad girl in the boarding house.

Harold notified me that his buddy at Ellington Field, Elmo Futrell, was shipping out with him. They made arrangements for Elmo's wife and me to meet at the Houston Bus Depot. We were told what the other wife planned to wear. They wanted for us to travel together from Houston to Big Spring, Texas. We met in plenty of time and we entered the bus together. I knew the moment I saw her that I liked her. As we sat on the bus as it left the station, Mildred Futrell and I hoped that we would be on a very successful venture.

Big Spring, Texas

Chapter Nine

On our way to Big Spring, Texas, from Houston, I knew that Mildred and I were going to be good friends. We were about the same size and of average appearance (both about 5' 5" tall and weighing between 108 lbs. to 115 lbs.) We were interested in learning about each other and we enjoyed talking about our home life and our families. Mildred and Elmo Futrell were raised on farms in Pineville, Louisiana. My parents were both raised on farms near Toledo, Ohio. When I was young, I spent my summer vacation visiting my aunts and uncles, staying for about a week from one farm house to another. I could play all day in the barn, watching the animals and climbing into the hay mows. I loved sitting up in trees, watching the birds fly into and out of the tree. I never needed anybody else to keep me happy on the farm. My uncles did like or seemed to like to take me with them on the farm wagons as they went out to the field to work. I liked to talk to them on the way.

I enjoyed the bus trip with Mildred. Our time together on the bus was fun. At first we talked a lot, but as we rolled along in the spacious West Texas countryside, we began to watch and study the scenery from the bus window. The ranches, farmland, dairy farms and the tumbling tumbleweeds were interesting to see as we went by. We forgot about talking to each other. I had heard of tumbleweeds, but I did not know they were large round bushes with the roots pulled out by the strong West Texas winds. When they tumbled gracefully past us, almost as high as the bus windows, I was amazed!

It was late in the afternoon before the bus arrived at Big Spring, Texas. The longer I was on the bus, the more my body began to ache. I hurt all over but I didn't want to complain. I thought when we got into our hotel room, I would be able to relax and feel better. Mildred and I went into the Settles Hotel which was near the bus station. We registered for a room and were happy to finally get settled for the night. The hotel was very modern with shops and services, everything a traveler needed. When we reached our room, I began to unpack my bags but I could not keep from moaning. I was hurting from all my aches and pain. I didn't know what to do about it. Mildred offered to go the pharmacy in the lobby of the hotel to ask what she could buy that would help me. I agreed because I felt I needed something. She came back to our room with a bottle of liniment. She suggested that I let her rub the liniment over my body.

I stretched out on my bed. Mildred rubbed the liniment carefully over my back, shoulders and arms and legs. I began to feel better. I thanked Mildred over and over for helping me. I was able to relax and I finally got to sleep. I used the liniment during the night to help me get back to sleep. The next morning, I phoned a downtown doctor for an appointment for me to see him as soon as possible. The nurse scheduled a checkup for me for that afternoon.

After our breakfast at the restaurant in the lobby, Mildred and I went to The Welcome Center for Army visitors located in the Hotel. We wanted to find a room to rent that would not be too far from the downtown area. The volunteers at the center were eager to help us. We decided to rent a room in a small house, near downtown Big Spring, owned by a middle-aged lady who lived alone. It would be easy for me to walk to the doctor's appointment from there. We walked to see the house. We liked the neighborhood and when the landlady greeted us at the door, she seemed OK. Our bedroom was small, but it was next to the living room, near to the front door, and separated from the rest of the house. The bathroom was near to our room. After the lady showed us around her home, we began to unpack our stuff. She gave us permission to call our husbands from there.

When it was time to go for my doctor's office, we left in plenty of time. It seemed good to walk into town. The doctor said I was in good health. He told me some women have arthritis only during pregnancy. From the doctor's office, Mildred and I walked around the downtown area. We realized Big Spring was a very prosperous town. A lot of the stores were elegant with many beautiful and expensive things in the windows.

Mildred and I both hoped our stay in Big Spring, Texas would be longer than the other places we had stayed as we followed our husbands. We planned to stay until our men graduated as officers of the Army on July 14, 1943. We did not look for jobs there. I was expecting our baby and Mildred didn't feel the need to get a job. We had a relaxing and happy time together. We laughed a lot! Our husbands called us almost every day from the base. We each talked to our mate and each day we tried to get our man to say, "I love you". It was a game we played but they never would say it because they didn't want any of the men around them to hear them mention those three little words.

One of the first things Harold told me was that he had made an appointment for me with one of the best doctors on the base. I had heard that the best OB doctors and pediatricians in all of Texas were on the staff at Big Spring Air Base. I rode the bus to the base many times in the 3 months I was there. I was happy and satisfied with the doctors at the base. I felt that everything was going fine for me!

Mildred and I learned our way around Big Spring in a very short time. We heard about a school nearby where we could go to watch sport games and other entertainment. We walked to the elementary school and asked in the office about visiting the school. They said we could check into the office any time we wanted to visit. They said we could also pay to eat lunch in the cafeteria if we wished. We were told by our landlady that we could not cook in her kitchen. We bought a good breakfast in town, ate a great lunch five days a week at the school and had fresh vegetables and snacks for supper. On Saturdays we were invited to join a cadet wives club at the Settles Hotel. It was a fun group and we looked forward to Saturdays. We all paid for our own lunch. They ordered the food from the hotel restaurant. Times were good for us!

We did not like our landlady. She hated the Mexicans and colored people in Big Spring. She would sit and talk with us, in the evening, in her living room. Mildred and

I hated listening to her tell us how she would order 'those people" to step off the sidewalk when she approached them. She would tell us how mean she could be to them at other times. I don't know if it was because we did not like her or because we wanted so much to do some cooking, but there came a time when we were so hungry for bacon, lettuce and tomato sandwiches, we bought those items at the store and when our landlady was snoring loudly and we thought she was sound asleep, we tiptoed into the kitchen (right next to her bedroom) and fried the bacon and made our sandwiches. They tasted so good! (I guess we thought she couldn't hear us or that she couldn't smell anything.)

The next morning, a knock came on our bedroom door. Our landlady told us, in a very nasty way, that we had to move out that day. What a rude awakening! She knew that we had been cooking in her kitchen that night and she was very upset. We dressed quickly and without much conversation, Mildred and I walked downtown to the Cadet Service Center to find another room. We didn't like that lady anyway. The room we chose was farther away from town, but there was an officer and his wife living there while looking for a house to rent. There were two young women bible students sharing a room. There was a room for us and also a spare room they rented to families of cadets when needed. The home was owned by an officer and his wife from the base. It was a great house! The volunteers at the Cadet Welcome Center recommended it highly.

Finally, when we had our plans to rent the room finalized, we went back where we lived to move out. We were not happy to face the job of packing up our things. We really didn't want to face that woman, not even one more time. We did have fun getting our clothes together. We tried on each others outfits. When Mildred tried on a suit jacket of mine, she couldn't get either arm into the sleeve. To our amazement, both sleeves were stapled shut! Later when she opened my pretty umbrella, a lot of confetti fell out all over the bedroom! My thought was, "What's going on here?" Then I remembered my bosses in Houston liked to play tricks on me. We laughed heartily as I told Mildred a lot of stuff they did to me in fun while I worked there. We both decided they did this to my jacket and my umbrella which I used on a rainy day. Perhaps the weather turned clear and beautiful, and I carried them home at the end of the day. We also laughed hard and were very noisy so that our landlady would think we were two very happy people.

All of a sudden, while we were packing, I remembered what was missing and not in my bedroom, when I moved from Houston to Big Spring. I left behind my beautiful powder-blue suit jacket and skirt. I loved the outfit and I wore it a lot in Texas. I had spilled stuff on it. It was getting dirty often and it couldn't be cleaned up properly any more. I had taken it to a dry cleaner in Houston to be dyed navy blue. No wonder it wasn't in my bedroom in Houston. Suddenly, I wasn't in a very happy mood any more. Mildred sympathized with me and we began to think of ways to get my precious suit back. I didn't know the name of the dry cleaning company. One of the two ladies I lived with in Houston was more responsible than the other. If I could think of her name and address, I could send her money to pay the cleaning bill and the postage and ask her to send my navy blue suit to me in Big Spring. I had no idea how to get back the suit I wore when we left the wedding reception for our honeymoon.

After that, Mildred and I packed in a hurry. We purposely left the room with overflowing junk in the waste basket, the confetti from my umbrella and all the stuff we didn't want was a mess all over the room. I would never do that but we were making a statement to that landlady. We were young and spiteful. As we left the house for the last time, we closed the front door with an extra loud bang and hurried to catch the bus to our new home.

I don't remember the bus ride or carrying our luggage to our new place. I don't remember moving into our room or sleeping there our first night. Maybe I worried about leaving the room in such a mess or how to get my honeymoon suit, now dyed navy blue, from the cleaners. Maybe I was just too tired to think about anything. That next day, as soon as we could, we began to unpack. I went through my papers, paid bill receipts, letters from home and everything I had in my luggage. I needed to find the name of the dry cleaner in Houston and also the name and address of the people I rented from there. Finally I found the information I needed and I became anxious to get to the Cadet Welcome Center at the Settles Hotel to talk to the volunteers for their advice about the best way to get my, now navy blue suit, sent to me from the cleaners.

As soon as we could, Mildred and I took the bus to downtown Big Spring. It was good to be back in town! The volunteers at the Welcome Center suggested that I write to the ladies I roomed with in Houston, to ask them if they would arrange to get my suit sent to the Cadet Center at The Settles Hotel. When the suit arrived, they would call me and hold it until I could pick it up. The plan sounded good to me. I thanked them for their help. Before we left the hotel, Mildred and asked if the cadet wives still met for lunch on Saturday. They did and we left the hotel planning to return to meet the girls next Saturday. We decided to walk over to the grade school to see our friends, the cooks and servers, in the cafeteria.

We talked about planning to take the bus a few days a week to eat the good hot food they served.

On the bus trip back to our room, we wished we were living closer to the downtown area! That night we talked, in the living room, with the bible students after they returned from their classes. We enjoyed our discussions with them! It was interesting to hear the things they learned about the bible. One quote they said quite often, "Once a child of God, always a child of God", bothered me and still does. To this day I will ask different bible leaders about that phrase. The girls were sure if you are ever a child of God, God will see that you are in heaven with him. I had not been attending church regularly. I missed not spending Sunday mornings in church. I prayed daily and I felt God was with me each day.

The young officer and his wife, who roomed upstairs near us until they found a house to buy, were busy a lot and we didn't see them very often. She was 17 years old, and demanded a lot of attention from her husband. She was also snobbish toward us. Mildred and I decided it was because she was an officer's wife and we were married to cadets. We did not enjoy being with her. I remember something that happened that made me feel very dumb and very responsible for her discomfort. Another officer and his wife were going to spend a day at the beach with this couple. The young wife was very excited to be going to the beach for the day. She had very fair skin and she worried about getting sunburned. I told her not to stay in the sun too long. I told her as long as the sun was not out, she wouldn't burn. I didn't know at that time that on a cloudy day, your skin will burn even if the sun is not shining. The sun did not come out all day and when they returned home, she was burned so badly I wanted to cry for her. She blamed me for her sunburn and I certainly felt it was my fault. She said she had been on the beach all day. I learned a lesson about the sun, the shade, and sunburn!

A few days later, our husbands phoned to tell us they were getting their first over-night pass. We were very happy and began making plans for those days. We told our landlord about Harold and Elmo both getting an upcoming leave and they suggested that if we wanted to use their kitchen to cook a dinner for our husbands while they were here, it would be fine with them. We were so thankful for the opportunity to cook for our men. We offered to clean, not only the dining room and the kitchen, but we insisted that we wanted to clean the whole house. The people we rented from arranged for the other renters not to use the downstairs that night. We had a wonderful meal and a perfect evening. All four of us cleaned up the dining room and kitchen that night. The next day after our husbands went back to the Air Base, Mildred and I spent hours happily cleaning and scrubbing everything in the whole house. We both enjoyed the feeling of being a housewife, if only for that short time.

Mildred and I spent most of our time in our bedroom, writing letters to our families and to our friends back home. I wrote to the women where I lived in Houston to ask them to help me by arranging with the dry cleaner to send my suit to the Welcome Center in Big Spring, Texas. I sent enough money to pay for their time, the dry cleaner's bill, and the postage. Finally my navy blue suit arrived at Big Spring. I certainly was happy to receive it.

Each day we talked about a lot of things. I told Mildred, in detail, about when I arrived in San Antonio and lived with all the cadet wives on the third floor of the boarding house. My life there was very interesting. I told her about the cadet wife whose life was featured with two other cadet wives and their husbands in the nationally published Ladies Home Journal. I told her also about the conversation we had one night about how our lives had changed after war was declared on December 7, 1941. One cadet wife said her life after December 1941, and especially when her husband went to war, was like a broken egg, all mixed up. We both agreed with her and we talked about how we felt at that time. We both wished that we were living downtown now. Life was better for us there! We missed being close to all the fun times we had when we were downtown.

My arthritis, with a small ache in my jaw, was bothering me, but vitamins and an aspirin once or twice a day helped a lot and the pain didn't keep me from having fun. I had an appointment with my doctor at the base soon and I would tell him about my arthritis. Mildred and I talked to our husbands whenever they phoned us. We tried to always be two happy people, and we were! We enjoyed this wonderful friendship we had. It had been a few weeks since we moved into this nice home, but we did not like taking the bus so often. We couldn't do anything we wanted to do without transportation. Finally there came a time, when we decided to take the bus to the Cadet Welcome Center at the hotel to see what housing was available near downtown.

At the Welcome Center we were told about a very nice large, older home near the downtown area, owned by an elderly lady. The volunteers assured us it would be just right for us. We walked to see the house and the neighborhood. We liked everything we saw! We knew when we talked to the owner that she would be a perfect grandma for us. She showed us our bedroom. It was a big room at the front of the house next to a very large living room. She said we could use the living room any time as a part of our apartment. Also, we could use her kitchen for our breakfast. We decided to move in as soon as possible! The landlady lived in the rear of the house. Her living space was very large. She had three large bedrooms, (one nice extra bedroom we could rent if we had company) a great dining room, a huge kitchen, an extra bath room, a large pantry, and a back porch.

After we moved, the pain in my mouth began to bother me more. It still wasn't much of a pain. A few drinks of cold water helped a lot. We loved being close to everything. We walked to town to window shop almost every day. We ate a hot lunch every week day and spent Saturdays with the cadet wives. Harold and Elmo called us almost every day and we both continued to try, in new and different ways, to get our husband to say those three little words "I Love You". Harold and Elmo were thankful that Mildred and I were so happy in our new home. Their schedules were different at the base, so Mildred and I made our own plans to visit our husband whenever he was able to see us at the base. It was also easy for them to visit us in downtown Big Spring whenever they had a one-day pass.

Our 'grandma' had a cute little granddaughter, about 10 years old. She came, often, to be in our room or the living room to talk to us. We enjoyed her time with us. We did a lot of fun things with her. We combed her hair and she combed ours. Mildred could plait, or braid, the girl's hair and she did that often for her. One day, just teasing the little girl, Mildred started talking with a German accent. I picked up on the game and answered Mildred, as best I could, with German words I remembered from my German classes I had in High School. The little girl's eyes got large. She pulled away from us. She was scared! (America was fighting Germany and she knew we were Germans!) She left us in a hurry that day and never came back to be with us. We spoiled a good friendship! We felt awful that we scared her but she was beginning to be more demanding of our time. We couldn't tell her not to come to see us so often. In the end, we felt it worked out Ok for us.

There were nice neighbors living next door to Grandma's house and they became our friends. The mother was about my mother's age. She and her husband had a very young married daughter, living at home, whose husband was stationed far away and was not able to come home very often. We never met him. We would stop to talk to the mother once in a while. She was concerned about both us and our life away from home. She was like a mother to us and helped us with any questions we had. I often saw her daughter, who worked at one of the shops downtown, at the air field with some of her girl friends. They had a group of soldiers they enjoyed visiting. I began to worry about her and the soldier she was so happy with. It was like a romance in progress! I worried about her marriage! I was so happy that I was near Harold and that we were not separated by the war!

I took the bus to the field for my doctor appointments. Whenever Harold could, he would meet me to see a good movie or any advertised shows and/or live entertainment. We saw Bob Hope while we were there. One thing that added to the movie or the entertainment was the enthusiasm (the hooting and laughter of the servicemen). The auditorium was always filled with service people who clapped and cheered longer and louder than at any show in the city. I missed that enthusiastic excitement back home whenever I went to a movie during and after the war. All the time we lived there, grandma was always interested in listening to us and offering her advice if we asked for it.

As Harold's Graduation Day approached, my toothache became unbearable. On a Saturday night, I sat up in the rocking chair in our living room all night. Nothing helped the pain and I could not sleep. When grandma, who always got up early, saw me sitting in the living room and asked "why", I told her about my toothache. She called her dentist as early as possible. He opened his office and met me there on that Sunday morning. He pulled that tooth! My arthritis and my toothache both disappeared within that day and I was never bothered again. Imagine that!

My parents and Harold's mother (his father couldn't come because he had to stay at his job in Toledo) and his brother, Kenny were coming the next Saturday, on the train from Toledo, for Harold's graduation as a Bombardier on July 15, 1943 (class of 43-10) at the Army Air Force Post Theatre. I had rented a room for our family at the Settles Hotel. I did not go with Mildred to the cadet wives luncheon that Saturday because I had too much to do to be ready for our parents that afternoon. Soon Mildred phoned me from the luncheon, telling me I should come down as soon as I could. She insisted that I come, but wouldn't tell me why. I finally told her "OK". When I arrived at their luncheon, the wives had planned a surprise baby shower for me. What a surprise!

Before I went to the train station to meet our family, I moved all my baby gifts to the rented room I had at the hotel. Oh the excitement of it all and the "Thank You," again and again, to friends who were so thoughtful. I never expected a shower. That made my day! I was so excited to show the baby things to the grandparents-to-be when we arrived at the hotel. They were very impressed and emotional about the shower gifts, and being in Texas for Harold's graduation.

The neighbor living next to us had insisted that my Mom and Dad stay with her while they were in Big Spring. I agreed to rent a room from her, and I also rented the extra room at grandma's house for Mother Frutiger and Kenny. We moved from the hotel the day after our family arrived. Before the graduation, my mother-in-law wanted to go shopping with me to buy a maternity dress for me. We went into downtown and we found a two-piece summer dress (not a maternity dress) that I really liked. It had a full skirt that Mom Frutiger said could be altered so that I could wear it now and it would fit me until our baby came. She was able to use my neighbor's sewing machine to alter it for me. Mom Frutiger worked at the Lion Store department store in Toledo as a seamstress in the suit and coat department. I wore it to the graduation and I felt I looked great that day. I thanked her for that! I thanked everyone for coming to Big Spring to be with me and Harold for this wonderful time in our life. I thanked my friends for taking care of our family. My next door neighbor and my mother became good friends. They corresponded and exchanged Christmas cards for years.

Harold was anxious and very excited to graduate. He was hoping he would be appointed Second Lieutenant in the Air Force rather than a Flight Officer in the Army as many in his class were expecting. We were all so happy and impressed when Harold stepped up to receive his wings from his Commanding Officer. He was commissioned Second Lieutenant in the Army of the United States, effective that day, July 15, 1943. It was truly a most fulfilling and emotional day for Harold and for me! We all enjoyed our time with our family for the rest of that day. The next day we said a sad goodbye to them at the train station. Harold reported for duty at the Air Base and I returned to my room as the proud wife of a Second Lieutenant in the Army Air Force.

Two weeks before he graduated, Harold was given a list of clothing he needed to purchase (and charge the bill) at a Big Spring Men's store. I went with him and it was fun to see how good he looked in his uniform. These clothes were basic for service overseas. At the base P.X. he was issued additional clothes he needed. We knew that after his graduation, he would be sent to an Army Air Force training school for new officers. We planned that would be when I would leave Big Spring and take the train to Toledo to live with my parents until our baby was born. The due date was December 7th. Harold's plan was to come to Toledo when our baby arrived.

When Harold left for his new training base, I had to leave Big Spring for Toledo. Mildred and Elmo had already moved on to their next adventure. As I said goodbye to my life as a cadet wife, it was with mixed emotions that I packed my things and got on that train to go home to be with my parents and to await our new baby. As the train pulled away from the station, I cried softly with an aching heart. I felt tired and alone and not certain of my future. At the same time I was excited and anxious to get to Toledo to be with my family and all my friends.

Baby Makes Three

Chapter Ten

On the train ride from Big Spring to Toledo Ohio, I was very pensive and quiet. I didn't want to talk to anyone. Most of the time I wanted to cry and I didn't know why. It was like I wanted to be alone with my feelings! I was sad a lot of the time. All of a sudden my thoughts would change and I would want to giggle about something funny or fun Mildred and I had together. I knew I would miss her in my life. It seemed I would be happy and then flip into a very sad mood. I felt like a basket case.

Finally as my baby moved gently inside me, I began to be concerned for my baby and my health also. I thanked God for our good health, for Harold and his success in the Air Force and his Second Lieutenant commission. I was happy our baby was on the way with only about three more months to wait. When I reached Toledo I would be with our families. I really was happy to be going home!

It was wonderful living at home with my family. Relatives and friends heard that I was there and many phoned or visited us. Harold's parents came over often. They invited us to visit with them at their small farm near Toledo. It was great to be with both families. We all missed Harold! We talked about our letters from him and everything he was doing in the Army Air Force. When he finished his training as a new officer he was commissioned to return to Big Spring as a bombardier instructor for advanced Cadets, American and Brazilian. I was happy he was back in Big Spring. I was very anxious to get there!

Every so often, ever since we were together, Harold would surprise me with a book he thought I would like. One day he sent me a book titled, Who Could Ask For Anything More written by Kay Smith, copyright 1943. Inside on the first page he had dated it in the upper right hand corner, "8-25-43". To the left of the next page he wrote, "To my Wife. A date I'll never forget, 8-25-38. Our first date." This was a great surprise and a treasured book I have on my bookshelf to this day.

All the time I was home, we went to church every Sunday morning and Mom always had a hot dinner ready for us in the oven when we came home from church. Time went by quickly for me. Baby showers were planned and I was excited to receive the darling baby gifts. We were often trying to think of names for our baby. My mother's sister, Aunt Lydia, suggested the girl's name, Sharon Kay. Harold and I earlier had decided, if we had a girl, we both liked the name, Carol Jean, and that was the name I was sure we would call her. (I had a bottle of good lotion with the name Carol Jean on it.) However, there were four Carols in our neighborhood and their mothers were always calling for them. I heard the name yelled out many times, day after day. One day when Harold called me on the phone, I told him I was beginning to get very tired of hearing the name, Carol. I asked him about Aunt Lydia's suggestion, Sharon Kay, and he liked it a lot. It was a new name to both of us. We did not know anyone by that name. William Arthur was to be the name if we had a boy!

It was getting closer to the arrival of our baby and I was getting very large. I gained 40 pounds from the 106 lbs. I weighed in Houston to the 146 lbs. I weighed when I went to the hospital for our baby. Harold's mom and dad always asked me to go with them whenever they went to the movies. Harold's Aunt Edna always went with us. Winter weather was with us and it was hard for me to get around but I always liked to go with them. When I talked to Harold on the phone, I didn't want to tell him how uncomfortable I was. He was always happy when I went with his parents. On Saturday, December 4th, I decided to go with Mom and Dad Frutiger to the movies even though I hadn't been feeling too well all day. I began to have cramps every once in a while during the movie but it wasn't anything to be concerned about.

When Harold's parents dropped me off at home after the movie, I went straight up to bed. My parents were both sleeping and I went right to sleep. I awoke with cramps that were coming harder and more often. I didn't know just when to call my parents. Finally I woke them up and before we went to the hospital, we sat at the kitchen table and each drank a cup of tea. My bag had been packed for a few days and with it and wearing our heavy winter clothes, we drove to the hospital about 2:00 A.M. on Dec, 5. Our baby, Sharon Kay, was born about 2:00 P.M. on December 5, 1943. It seemed like a very long wait with both of our families waiting in the waiting room, at Women and Children's Hospital on Summit Street in Toledo, Ohio.

At Big Spring, Harold was waiting anxiously for our baby to be born. The army's new rule was that a leave of absence would not be issued for the birth of a baby born away from the Big Spring area. A soldier could apply for a pass to be with his wife if their baby was born nearby. Harold wanted to try to get to Ohio for our baby's birth. He intended to buy a used car in Toledo and drive it back to Big Spring. His plan was to get his wife and his baby to live with him in Big Spring as soon as possible.

When my parents notified Harold that he had a baby daughter, he went to the Commanding Officer and asked for a pass to get home. He said his wife was in the hospital in Toledo and he needed to be there. The Commanding Officer quickly made out a pass for him. Harold thanked him and, with the signed papers in his hand, he hurried out the door. The officer called out to ask why his wife was in the hospital. Harold told him, we had a baby girl, as he hurried down the hall and out of the building.

I was kept a total of 12 days in the hospital, the usual time for the birth of a baby. (Years later, all US newspapers carried the headlines that in Europe the new mothers were being sent home in 5 days. All we women wondered how that could be! We felt we couldn't go home in 5 days!) After Sharon was born, while I was still in the hospital, I developed a serious bladder infection. When Harold arrived home, he spent as much time as he could with Sharon and me in the hospital. He also shopped for a good used car and finally bought one. He drove it around the hospital so I could see it from my hospital window.

The day before Harold needed to drive the car back to Big Spring, my doctor refused to release me from the hospital. I had a serious talk with the doctor about wanting to be home with my husband and our baby before he had to leave. Dr. Ward's answer was "NO". He told me I still had an infection. I told him, with my medicine, I was going home with my husband and our baby that day. I told him his father, our family doctor, would have released me. As he was leaving, my doctor stood at the door of my hospital room and told me I could go any way "I damn pleased." With that, he stormed out the door! I went home, happily, with my husband and our new baby.

Harold was coming down with a bad cold. He carried me upstairs to my bedroom. He stayed the night with us but he keep as far away from me and Sharon Kay as he could. He didn't want for either of us to catch his cold. From my upstairs bedroom window the next morning, I heard his car pull out of the driveway as he headed for Texas. Knowing that he was sick with a terrible cold, and that he had winter driving weather ahead of him, I worried about him. I was feeling very sad how my homecoming with my husband and our baby had turned out! I put my face into my pillow and cried for a long time. Nothing had worked out as I planned!

Sharon was in her bassinet next to my bed. I knew she needed me now! As I turned from crying into my pillow to seeing what I could do for our baby, I began my life as a mother. I knew that Harold and I were not just a couple, two people, any more. We were a family of three! My parents were very attentive to me and Sharon Kay. Both my Mom and my Dad had plenty of good advice for what should be done for our baby. I knew nothing about caring for a baby. It wasn't too many days before she was awake and crying a lot. My parents said she had colic. We were taking turns walking her to sleep. Some time later, Dr. Ward said we needed to supplement a bottle for her. I had trouble finding the correct food for her. We found that SMA (a popular brand of canned baby milk) was great for her. She began to be happier and to sleep a lot! SMA was the first thing I told Harold to order a case for us when he found that not a druggist in Big Spring carried SMA.

We had many friends visiting to greet me and Sharon. Harold's parents came often. My relatives and Harold's family came. Also some of the women I worked with at Travelers Insurance called and came over. It seemed like there was never a dull moment. When we came home from the hospital, Christmas was just about a week away and I was wishing Harold could be home with us for our first Christmas with our new baby.

Harold's trip back to Big Spring was a horrid trip for him. His cold was very bad and his car's heater didn't work. He was shivering and freezing in the cold weather. He knew he had a fever. He drove wrapped in a blanket all the way to Texas, just stopping to buy gas. As soon as he arrived at the Air Force Base, he went right to the hospital. They admitted him and kept him there until he was well!

I helped my family get ready for Christmas. We celebrated as best we could and then it was New Year's Eve. I was glad for New Year's Day, 1944, to arrive. Harold phoned as often as he could and we began to plan a date for us to leave for Big Spring. Dr. Ward said Sharon Kay should be at least 10 weeks old before we left for Big Springs. We set February 7, 1944 as the day for baby Sharon and me to take the train to Texas. She would be 10 weeks old then. I decided to listen to my doctor this time. For Harold it was 'the sooner the better'! He had some friends he wanted me to meet. He had spent a lot of time with, Ted and Marge Gilleland. Ted had graduated as a bombardier in the same class as Harold but his wife did not join him until he was assigned there after graduation. Marge liked to cook and they would often invite Harold to come to eat with them. Sometimes they would invite several of the single officers from the base to join them for supper.

My mother and Harold's mother decided to travel with me on the train. I was happy for that! We had sleeper compartments across the aisle from our seats. We had four seats on the train and we turned them to face each other. We had all our bags under our seats and around our feet. We always needed to get something from one of the bags and it was very nerve-wreaking. It took 3 days to get to Big Spring. When we arrived at the train depot, Harold was there. Oh what a joy to be together!

He had rented a large, old one-story farm house for two nights. It was situated in a cluster of small cottages in an old Travel Park. Harold explained that most of the cottages were rented by soldiers and their families from the Air Force Base. He said we would be there for only two nights. He had been lucky enough to rent a new large one-story mansion, located on a 17,000 acre ranch about 5 miles outside of Big Spring. The owner had a factory in town but he was working for a large factory in California where war products were manufactured. This ranch house could only be rented to an officer at the Air Base. Harold felt that he was lucky to be there at the right time to get it. The price was right!

It was unusually cold for West Texas when we arrived and we hurried to get settled in the farm house for the night. Our two mothers slept in the larger bedroom with baby Sharon in her bassinet in their room. It got so cold during the night in that drafty old house. They began to wonder if Sharon would freeze. They checked and she was so cold, they finally took her in bed with them. The next morning we toured Big Spring and the Air Force Base. We were impressed with the officer's quarters there. Harold drove out to show us the ranch house he had rented. I was anxious to move out there. After we said goodbye to our mothers at the train station the next morning, we packed our things and moved out to the ranch.

We were happy living out in the country. There was a huge dairy farm across the road and the scenery was beautiful. During the day, hundreds of cows grazed out in the pasture surrounded by a high fence. I loved to sit on our front porch and watch the changing view of the cows in the distance. We had three porches on the house. One was a large porch on the front, a smaller porch off the living room on the right side, and a small porch on the left side with a door to a large back bedroom. I put Sharon Kay for her naps in her bassinet on the small porch outside the living room. She loved to sleep outside. When the pilots from the air field learned that Harold and his wife and baby were living in that ranch house, they would dive down and tip their wings to us and then dash high into the sky. That was a great thrill for me!

Harold knew that the ranch owner had not been able to get the neighbor owners to sign for the electricity wires to go over their property and that we would get our electric power from a wind charger high on a scaffolding outside our back door. He also was told that we had a trailer with a huge tank they attached to our car to carry water from the owner's factory to put into the well each night because he had trouble with every well he dug. They all went dry. We learned that we had just enough water to get through each day. He needed to bring another trailer with water from town each night.

We had about 19 base plugs around the house and beautiful light fixtures and lots of lamps, but we only had electricity when the wind blew hard. Even then, we always needed to use hurricane lamps to read by. We played cards using a hurricane lamp and sometimes did our evening dishes with a hurricane lamp. We had enough light for one outlet but if we turned on another light we didn't have enough light for either area. Even then, we felt we had a good deal renting this home and we had a great house to live in. A little bothersome but we were happy.

Soon after we moved in, Harold rented the large back bedroom, with the small porch attached, to a flight pilot at the Air Force Base. He and his wife moved in. Their home was east of Toledo, near Clyde, Ohio. Myron and Rosie Welty were good neighbors while they lived there with us. That was the start of a life-long friendship. The Weltys had their own bathroom. We shared the kitchen. They ate in the breakfast room and we had the large dining room next to our living room. Sometimes Harold invited a couple from the base to play cards at our dining room table. We learned to play Bridge there by the light of a hurricane lamp.

As soon as we could, we contacted the Gillelands. They wanted us to come for Sunday dinner. They were anxious to meet me and see our baby. I really enjoyed meeting them and spending that time with them. They lived in a converted garage. The owner, a widow, had her car in the garage along side their dining table with an ornate buffet along the wall. Their kitchen was built along the back wall of the garage. They needed to go past the owner's car to get to their bathroom. Ted and Marge lived there all the time they were in Big Spring.

Later we decided to have a potluck cookout at the ranch. Harold invited a large group of people from the base. Ted and Marge Gilleland were there. We had many single men, also men and their wives. Some single men brought a date. Most of the soldiers did not have an apartment or a house where they could entertain like that, so it was a treat for all of us. We spread the food on a large trailer at the back of the house. It was one of the highlights of our stay. Another highlight, and a great memory, was on another day when the fence around the Dairy Farm broke and I saw cows staring into our windows. What a surprise! We had cows all around our house! Sharon and I waved to them from inside the window and it was great fun for both of us.

A few times Harold was able to take us for a planned visit back to where Mildred and I lived, to see Grandma and her neighbor next door. He dropped us off and returned later too pick us up. Baby Sharon even got a bath at the neighbor's house. They knew about our water problem at the ranch. One day she invited me to come to be a fourth player for a Bridge game. I enjoyed that day. Sharon took her nap on their front porch and I felt that I was part of the family.

About a month or so after Myron and Rose Welty moved to live with us on the ranch, Harold was returning home, as he did each day, with a trailer-load of water to be put into our well. One of the tires on the truck blew out about two or three miles from home, and he had to let the water out in the field along the side of the road to get the trailer home. Needless to say, he had had it! He was very angry! There was not enough water or electricity for us to have a peaceful living in that beautiful ranch house. The next day he rented a small apartment in town. We moved as soon as we could. Myron and Rosie moved to town too. They found a place to rent not far from where we planned to live.

Our apartment was on the right side of a small house divided in half. Our living room was the original living room. The dining room was our bedroom and we had the original kitchen. The back door was from the kitchen with 3 steps pushed up to the outside of the house. We shared the bathroom with the renters on the other side of the house. We moved late one night after Harold came home from work.

It was late when we got settled with our bed made and Sharon's crib ready for her in our bedroom. We did not unpack our suitcases that night. When I woke up late that next morning, Harold had left for work before dawn. My eyes fell on a shadow on the wall from the sunshine coming in the window. I could see something moving up and down the sides and across the top of my suitcase, filled with clothes, which was in our bedroom at the foot of Sharon's bed. I found out later that they were called 'palmetto bugs' (known as 'roaches' in Ohio). When Harold turned on the light in the kitchen that morning, those bugs were scampering all over to get out of sight. Again, I was very proud of Harold and his job before the war. He sold cleaning supplies and was always able to know the right product for any cleaning job. When he came home from work that day, he had the right stuff to rid us of those pests. I learned that a lot of people down there lived with them all the time. They won't hurt you! We also learned that in the summer, it was so hot some people would sprinkle their beds with cold water so they could sleep.

Times were good for us. Sharon Kay was growing up quickly and learning more things every day. There was a rocker in our living room and I loved to rock her. My parents sent a new stroller for Sharon and she could sit in it at first, then reach the floor with her toes and very soon she was able to move it around the house. Sharon and I became a team. I would wheel her around the neighborhood in her stroller. The houses were small and most had a vegetable garden on their lot. We walked to the grocery store and she always had grocery bags tucked around her as I pushed the stroller home. She was walking at 11 months and by Christmas time she always walked around the house without the walker. The one Christmas present my Dad picked out for Sharon was in the box of gifts the Toledo people sent to us. It was a doll with a long, full skirt. He thought it was the cutest thing he had ever seen. It was a baby with a white face but when you turned it over and the full skirt fell over that side, it was a black baby. When Sharon Kay opened that package, she started to cry, and nothing would quiet her and nothing would stop her crying until we put it away. Needless to say, we hid it in the closet.

One thing Sharon loved to do and I loved to watch her. She would go the front door in her walker, turn around as fast as she could and race through our bedroom and into the kitchen. She would hit the screen door (which I always kept locked) as hard as she could and bounce back in her walker and we would both laugh. One day the back door was not locked and I watched her go flying out the door, right over the three steps and landed on her side with the stroller on top of her. That's when the walker was put in the back of the closet along with the hated Christmas present my dad sent to Sharon for Christmas when she was one year old!

By this time Sharon was walking with me around the neighborhood and to the store. She loved to walk without holding my hand and she always wanted to hold a small package of groceries on the way home. Sometimes she would be tired of walking but she would never complain. She would keep on walking and if I didn't see that she was getting tired she would finally sit down and we would wait until she was ready to go again. Harold and I had a lot of fun with her. We often wondered what we talked about before we had her. The three of us would drive to the park on the day he wasn't working at the Air Base. We also drove the other side of Big Spring to visit the Gillelands. Ted and Marge were great friends. We also liked to spend time with Paul and Morelan Powel. They had a little girl, Judy Kay, the same age as Sharon. The two little girls would crawl on the floor a lot, just following each other around. We adults always laughed a lot whenever we were together. Some friends seem to bring out humor in others. We laughed about everything. They would be on either side of our car as we slowly pulled away from the curb, in order to get another laugh or two before we said goodbye.

Sharon Kay and I were invited to Judy Kay's first birthday party. Paul was on a baseball team from the Air Base and they had many friends I did not know. (We seldom went to watch their games.) There were many little children and babies and all the mothers at Judy Kay's birthday party. It was really a great party. Sharon was very shy and did not want to leave my side. She stayed next to me during the party. They took a group picture of all the little ones sitting together on the floor. Sharon did not want to leave my side, but she is in the picture! That was Sharon's first birthday party.

Once, very soon after we moved to town, I left Sharon Kay with the lady in the apartment next to us. I wanted to drive with Harold to the Air Base so I could have the car for the day. When we reached the parking lot, I hoped that he would stop at the driveway and walk from there. I was a very new driver! Instead, he pulled right and parked between two parked cars. He kissed me goodbye and entered the building at the mess-hall door. I knew I would have trouble getting out from between the cars and not hit the building behind me. I looked both ways and out the back window and with nothing in sight, I backed out. I hit something with a loud bang, water started engulfing my car, and Harold came running, got into the driver's seat and drove the car out to the street. What I hit was a large tank of fuel oil, held high upon two brick walls. What I thought was water around my car was the fuel oil. That day in the mess hall, everyone knew it was Harold's wife who made them eat cold cuts because of no fuel for the cook stoves! The only thing that soothed me and Harold, too, was that the Commanding Officer had the same accident the week before. After my damage, tall cement posts were added around the tank of fuel so that it couldn't be knocked down.

My favorite thing to do was for Sharon and me to walk over to spend some time with Rosie Welty. Myron and Rosie had no children when they lived in the ranch house with us. Later, when they lived in town, they had a little girl and I was there quite often to help her and give her encouragement with problems with her new baby. Sharon Kay liked to visit there too. She loved that little baby. The Weltys moved on to a new base before we left Big Springs. They stopped to say goodbye to us at our place. Their car was loaded with stuff they were moving with them. Goodbyes are normal when you live in an army town, but they are always hard to do.

One night while Harold and all the others instructors where up in the air flying with their students practicing night bombing, a tragic accident happened. Harold told me when he came home that night, that two airplanes had collided in mid-air and all the crews flying up there watched in horror as both planes burst into flames and fell to the ground. All the crews returned to the hanger immediately.

None of the men flying up there that night knew which two of the planes crashed. From the hangar, the men waited anxiously for each plane to land. Harold said they knew that when only three planes were still up, only one more would be returning. He was relieved when his best friend, Paul Powel, was with that crew that returned! One of the instructors not coming back had been married that weekend and his new bride was staying somewhere in Big Spring. We were very sad for her, even though we didn't know her and didn't know where she was staying.

The day came when both Harold and Paul Powel received their orders to leave Big Spring and report to Lincoln, Nebraska for their flight crew assignments. The war was ending and most of the instructors were to be sent overseas to help end the war. We packed our belongings into our car and, all three of us, waved goodbye to our home in Big Spring and, with mixed emotions, drove to Lincoln.

Clovis, New Mexico and
The End Of The War

Chapter Eleven

While we were waiting for Harold's orders to arrive for his next assignment, he was given a short leave from Big Spring Air Force base. It was in early March of 1945 and we decided it would be a perfect time to fly to Toledo, Ohio. We would be home very close to Easter, and it would be wonderful to be able to spend some time with our parents for an early Easter celebration!

Sharon enjoyed the time with her grandparents but we did not have time to see many of our friends before we needed to return to Texas. One day the three of us went on a tour of the large department stores in downtown Toledo. It had been a long time since Harold and I had been shopping in Toledo. Sharon loved all the toys in each of the stores. I went into the Millinery Department to look at ladies hats. I found just the right hat, a darling, small white straw hat. Women wore hats everywhere....

to church, to the theater, to shop, to visit, etc. This was my new Easter Bonnet!

As we walked from one store to B.R. Bakers Men's Store, all three of us, Harold with Sharon Kay in his arms, stopped outside the store to watch the employees striking for better wages and/or better working conditions. They were noisy and rather scary. A few other people were standing with us as we all watched as the picketing people circled in an oblong circle which kept anyone from entering the store. A few men from inside the store stood at the door looking out. Finally Harold, in his army uniform, with Sharon still in his arms, began to walk through the striking workers. I followed him. They allowed us to enter the store. We greeted the owners and the employees inside and then began to look around the store. Harold chose the items he wanted to buy. We purchased them and wished everyone there that the demonstration would soon by over. We went outside through the picket line without any trouble. My heart was beating a mile a minute!

Soon our short visit to Toledo came to an end and we returned to Big Spring. There we learned that Harold was assigned to Lincoln, Nebraska with the possibility of training with a crew for an overseas tour of duty. On the way to Lincoln, Harold and I talked about the changes we might face in our life. Harold said he and Paul were anxious to get into a fighting crew and go overseas. I told him that Morelan and I had talked and we were both sad that the good life we had in Big Spring was over. I said I hoped the Japanese war was soon over, and we could get back into our little house on Harris Street in Toledo!

When we reached the Cornhuskers Hotel in Lincoln, Nebraska, the Powels were already there. While they waited for us to arrive, they decided to call the Presbyterian Church nearby to ask about two rooms for us to rent, hopefully in the same home. The organist at the church said that she and her husband had two rooms upstairs in their home that we could rent.

We drove directly from the hotel to their home, and after talking to the owners and seeing their neat little house we moved in. It was a perfect set-up for us. At the top of the steps was an open room. There were a couple of chairs and a card table and four chairs which Paul and Morelan and Harold and I enjoyed playing cards every night. Judy Kay and Sharon Kay colored in their coloring books and we read books to them during the day. We shared the only bathroom with the owners. It was at the foot of the stairs on the first floor. Upstairs, opposite the stairway, on the back wall, were our two bedrooms. Our children each played a lot, alone with their own toys, in their family bedroom.

We were offered the use of their kitchen for our meals. It worked fine for the six of us. One meal we were excited to have together was the prime steak Paul and Morelan had brought from their parents farm in Illinois. Paul and Harold had gone golfing that morning and we wives were happy to prepare a great meal for all of us when they returned.   When it was time for Morelan to drive to get them at the golf club, I planned to have everything ready for us when they came home. I always was very proud of my wonderful, lump-free gravy. My only problem was that I did not know how to fix steak. They were very late getting home. Everything was ready but the steak and I decided to begin to fry it. When they finally returned home, Morelan was upset with the men because she had to wait so long for them. All the food I made was delicious, except the steak was just too tough. However, the gravy was the best I had ever made! I was embarrassed about the too done steak.

We knew our stay there would be short and within two weeks our men received their orders to ship out to Clovis, New Mexico. They went on an Army troop train. The plan was for Morelan and I and the two girls to drive to Clovis in Powel's car. Our landlords were sorry to see us go. They helped us with loading our suitcases, big boxes and lots of stuff into her car. Morelan and I knew that we would not be able to get everything into the car, but the man and his wife were sure we could get it all in. We tried every way to pack it in and after many times with something we couldn't get into the car, they decided that it would not fit. They helped us repack a couple of boxes to be mailed ahead to the Officers Club in Clovis. They took care of that detail of mailing our stuff for us. With a car load of stuff, two tired kids, and two very exhausted mothers, we thanked them for all of their help and for our wonderful stay with them in their home. As we pulled away from the curb, we began our next adventure, hoping it would be the best one yet!

It was later than we had expected, but we were on our way and we knew we would make it to Portales, New Mexico in time to meet our men. They had notified us of the address in Portales where we would all be staying for a few nights until we had a place to live in Clovis. Portales was just a short distance south of Clovis, New Mexico.

On our way we stopped for gas and the gas station owner was excited about President Eisenhower being in town that day. He was sure we would want to stay to see our president in the parade. He couldn't understand why we were in such a big hurry to leave. We finally got on our way to New Mexico.

After two days in Portales, we were able to move into a motor home park in Clovis, where most rooms were rented to the air base service men and their families. The

Powels and Harold and I each had a room and bath. We had a large new garbage can. We added ice to it as needed to keep our milk and food from spoiling. While we were there we enjoyed the company of others living there. One bright sunny day we heard a terrible earth shaking noise. It couldn't be thunder.... there was not a cloud in the sky. We were very puzzled. We all ran to the railroad siding near our motor home. We thought maybe there had been a train accident. Nothing was visible on the tracks. It was puzzling to all of us. Much later, we learned that the first atom bomb was dropped near there in New Mexico!

Harold found a small one bedroom apartment that he was able to rent. He felt it was much better for us than where we were living. It was on the property of a two story farm home with a run down neighborhood across the alley from their home. They had a couple of wives of servicemen living in their home. They had turned their garage into a home about like the Gillilands had in Big Spring. Behind the garage was a room where they had all the home canned fruit and vegetables on shelves at the end of the room. A refrigerator was at the left of the door entering the food storage room. To the right was a shower. Behind the shower on the right side was the toilet, right next to the canned fruit. Behind this room was the room Harold rented. It was a converted chicken coop. We had our own door into the chicken coop, with a kitchen at the front and one nice bedroom to the back. What we both liked about this apartment was the large fenced yard that was a good place for Sharon to play. It was one half of the chicken yard. Every morning the rooster stood on our bedroom window and crowed. We shared the bathroom in the food pantry with the man and his wife who rented the garage. When we used the shower it hit the refrigerator and got it wet. We didn't think we would be there too long and never found a better place for us!

Epilogue

We know that this book ended abruptly due to our mom's death. After the war, Mom and Dad moved back to the little house on Harris Street. Later, they had three more children, Nancy, Joyce and Hal. Dad continued in the maintenance supply business and eventually, Mom and Dad started their own maintenance supply company, Tiger Products.

Mom and Dad kept in touch with many of the army friends mentioned in this book. They shared many happy memories from those years and helped Mom to recall some of the stories.

Mom and Dad were married for 58 years and had 12 grandchildren and 14 great grandchildren. Throughout their life together, Mom continued to travel with Dad on their many adventures throughout the United States and abroad.

Mom left us with many warm memories of a life well lived. We know that she would be so happy to see her story in print. This book, along with her love, is her legacy to her family.

Sharon, Nancy, Joyce, and Hal